100
Mexican Dishes

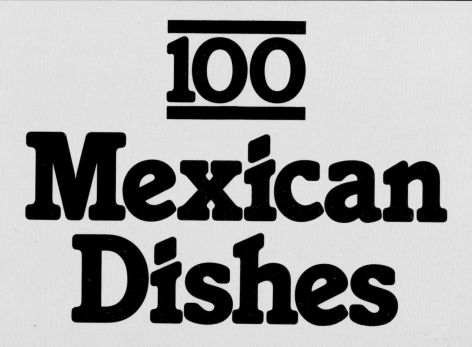

100
Mexican Dishes

Edited by
Grace Teed Kent

octopus

Contents

NOTES
Standard spoon measurements are used in all recipes
1 tablespoon=one 15ml spoon
1 teaspoon=one 5 ml spoon
All spoon measures are level.

Fresh herbs are used unless otherwise stated. If unobtainable, substitute a
bouquet garni of the equivalent dried herbs, or use dried herbs instead but
halve the quantities stated.
Ovens and grills (broilers) should be preheated to the specified temperature
or heat setting.
For all recipes, quantities are given in metric, imperial and American
measures. Follow one set of measures only, because they are not
interchangeable.

First published 1983 by
Octopus Books Limited
59 Grosvenor Street, London W1

© 1983 Octopus Books Limited
Reprinted 1984

ISBN 0 7064 1887 5

Produced by Mandarin Publishers Ltd
22a Westlands Rd
Quarry Bay, Hong Kong

Printed in Hong Kong

Frontispiece: Mexican Vegetable Soup (page 8)
(Photograph: American Spice Trade Association)

Introduction

Colourful and vibrant, Mexican cooking is one of the oldest and varied cuisines in the world due to the country's size, geography and history. Basically, Mexican food is Indian food and before the Spanish invasion in 1519, the Aztecs and Mayans lived on wild game and turkey, fish, wild pigs, tropical fruit and vegetables, beans, chillies, peppers and chocolate. Corn, sacred to the Aztecs, was a basic ingredient used mainly to make the flat, unleavened bread called tortilla. Most foods were boiled, grilled (broiled) or eaten raw as the Indians used no fats or oils in their cooking. Then the Spaniards arrived and brought with them lard (shortening) for frying, sugar, onions, garlic, wheat flour, peaches, apricots, cinnamon, cumin, allspice, coriander, cloves and almonds.

The regional differences in Mexican cooking reflect the differences in climate and geography. Rugged mountain ranges run down the middle of the country. The land varies from dry and arid near the Texas Border, to grasslands along the coastline, to tropical rain forests in the Yucatan Peninsula.

In the arid northern states, wheat is grown instead of corn. Therefore tortillas are made mainly of wheat flour. Cattle are raised in this area, so plenty of beef is included in the diet.

In the central states, pork, poultry and goat are found, with plenty of fruits and vegetables. Along the coastline of the Gulf of Mexico and in Vera Cruz, fish and shellfish are abundant and are transformed into many exciting dishes. On the Pacific coast lies Jalisco, famous for freshwater fish and the world-famous drink, Tequila, made from the fermented liquid of the agave plant. Both coasts are tropical, producing exotic fruits and vegetables. Southern Mexico is popular for spicy stews, tamales and quesadillas. The humid Yucatan Peninsula is another seafood area, the home of fish marinated in lime juice. Panuchos are also a favourite in this area.

The Mexican pattern of eating is very different to ours. They eat as many as five meals a day. Most Mexicans start the day with an early small breakfast, *Desayuno*, of sweet breads and buns served with coffee or chocolate. A heartier breakfast is eaten mid-morning, including an egg dish such as Huevos Rancheros, fruit, beans, tortillas and coffee. In the city this breakfast is reserved for weekends, whereas it is a much-needed meal in rural farming areas.

Comida, the main meal, is served in the afternoon and may continue for several hours. This includes soup, rice or a tortilla dish, a main course of meat, poultry or fish with beans, sauce, salad, vegetables and tortillas. As vegetables are used in all the dishes, a vegetable side dish, as we know it, plays a less important role. A fruit or caramel cream dessert and coffee finishes the meal. Then it is time for a siesta. There is an early evening meal called *Merienda*, rather like high tea, with sweet breads, biscuits and chocolate. *Cena*, a supper-type meal, is served at about 10.00 pm, but this and *Merienda* are now merging into one larger meal.

An introduction to Mexican cooking would not be complete without a few words about chillies, a member of the pepper family. In Mexico there are 100 varieties to choose from, varying in colour and strength from mild to scorching hot. When handling fresh or canned chillies, never touch the skin around the eyes or any other sensitive skin without first washing your hands well with soap and water, as the volatile oil from the chilli will cause irritation and distress. In most authentic Mexican dishes, the chillies are often not seeded, but if you prefer a less-hot flavour it is always better to seed the chillies and remove the membranes inside as you would with a green pepper. The range of fresh chillies in Great Britain is generally poor, however, some canned chillies such as Anaheim and Jalapeno may be tracked down. In the United States, many of the Mexican varieties can be found. Chillies are available in other forms, such as chilli powder, chilli seasoning, chilli sauce and cayenne pepper. Until familiar with cooking with chillies, powder or sauce, add gradually to a dish and taste until the required heat.

A final word on tortillas and tacos. In Mexico the traditional taco is a fresh, soft tortilla rolled around a filling. In the United States, tacos are corn tortillas that have been folded over and fried until crisp to make half-moon shaped shells. These are then filled with a selection of beef or chicken filling, lettuce, cheese, beans, green chillies, tomato and sauce. They can be made at home (see recipes on page 40) or the shells are available ready-made in some good food shops and delicatessens.

Soups & Starters

Tortilla Soup

METRIC/IMPERIAL
2-3 corn tortillas (see page 40)
oil for frying
50 g/2 oz onion, chopped
1 × 100 g/4 oz can chopped green chillies or 2 fresh green chillies, chopped
1 litre/1¾ pints chicken stock
225 g/8 oz cooked chicken, chopped
salt
1 × 298 g/10 oz can tomatoes and green chillies or canned tomatoes only
1 tablespoon lime juice

AMERICAN
2-3 corn tortillas (see page 40)
oil for frying
¼ cup chopped onion
1 can (4 oz) chopped green chilies
4 cups chicken stock or broth
1 cup shredded cooked chicken
salt
1 can (10 oz) tomatoes and green chilies
1 tablespoon lime juice

Cut the tortillas into 1 cm (½ inch) strips. Heat a little oil in a frying pan, add the tortilla strips and fry until brown and crisp, or deep fry. Drain on kitchen paper towels.

Heat 2 teaspoons oil in a large pan, add the onion and fry until soft but not brown. Add the green chillies, chicken stock, chicken, salt to taste and tomatoes and chillies. Cover and simmer for 20 minutes. Stir in the lime juice.

To serve, pour into soup bowls and add the tortilla strips.
Cooking time: about 30 minutes
Serves 4

Chicken and Nut Soup

METRIC/IMPERIAL
1 litre/1¾ pints chicken stock
1 potato, cubed
25 g/1 oz lard
1 onion, chopped
25 g/1 oz blanched almonds or walnuts, chopped
175 g/6 oz cooked chicken, shredded
150 ml/¼ pint double cream
salt and freshly ground pepper
1-2 tablespoons chopped coriander leaves to garnish

AMERICAN
4¼ cups chicken stock or broth
1 potato, cubed
2 tablespoons shortening
1 onion, chopped
¼ cup chopped almonds or walnuts
¾ cup cooked, shredded chicken
⅔ cup heavy cream
salt and freshly ground pepper
1-2 tablespoons chopped coriander leaves for garnish

Place the stock in a large pan and bring to the boil. Add the potato and simmer for 10 to 15 minutes until just tender but not soft.

Meanwhile, melt the lard (shortening) in a frying pan, add the onion and nuts and fry until lightly browned. Transfer to a blender, add half of the chicken and reduce to a purée. Alternatively, pound the mixture to a smooth paste, using a pestle and mortar.

Add the purée to the soup with the remaining chicken and simmer gently for 1 minute. Lower the heat, stir in the cream, then bring just to boiling point. Add salt and pepper to taste. Serve hot, garnished with chopped coriander.
Cooking time: 25 minutes
Serves 4 to 6

Tortilla Soup
(Photograph: Old El Paso Products)

Albondigas Soup

METRIC/IMPERIAL

2 sticks celery, cut
  into 1 cm/½ inch
  dice
1 large onion, cut into
  1 cm/½ inch dice
2 carrots, cut into
  1 cm/½ inch dice
1 green pepper,
  cored, seeded and
  cut into 1 cm/
  ½ inch dice
150 ml/¼ pint tomato
  sauce
1 bay leaf
1.6 litres/2¾ pints
  beef or chicken
  stock
1½ teaspoons salt
2 tablespoons
  coriander leaves
¼ teaspoon white
  pepper
1 clove garlic,
  crushed
½ teaspoon dried
  oregano
Meatballs:
750 g/1½ lb lean
  minced beef
2 eggs, beaten
25 g/1 oz coriander
  leaves
1 clove garlic,
  crushed
½ teaspoon ground
  cumin
½ teaspoon salt
freshly ground
  pepper

AMERICAN

2 stalks celery, cut
  into ½ inch dice
1 large onion, cut into
  ½ inch dice
2 carrots, cut into
  ½ inch dice
1 green pepper,
  seeded and cut into
  ½ inch dice
⅔ cup tomato sauce
1 bay leaf
7 cups beef or chicken
  stock or broth
1½ teaspoons salt
2 tablespoons
  coriander leaves
¼ teaspoon white
  pepper
1 clove garlic,
  minced
½ teaspoon dried
  oregano
Meatballs:
1½ lb lean ground
  beef
2 eggs, beaten
½ cup coriander
  leaves
1 clove garlic,
  crushed
½ teaspoon ground
  cumin
½ teaspoon salt
freshly ground
  pepper

Place all the soup ingredients in a large pan.
Bring to the boil and simmer the soup for about
20 minutes.

Meanwhile make the meatballs: mix the
beef, eggs, coriander, garlic, cumin, salt and
pepper together (the mixture will be wet).
Shape into 25 g/1 oz balls and put on a rack in a
roasting pan. Cook in a preheated moderate
oven (180°C/350°F, Gas Mark 4) for 15 to 20
minutes.

Place the meatballs in the soup and simmer
for about 10 minutes.
Cooking time: about 40 minutes
Serves 6 to 8

Mexican Vegetable Soup

METRIC/IMPERIAL

1 litre/1¾ pints beef
  stock
1 litre/1¾ pints water
1 × 225 g/8 oz can
  tomato sauce
2 tablespoons finely
  chopped onion
1¼ teaspoons
  crushed thyme
  leaves
1 clove garlic,
  crushed
1 teaspoon salt
225 g/8 oz chuck
  steak, cut into 1 cm/
  ½ inch cubes
½ teaspoon whole
  black peppercorns
4 whole cloves
225 g/8 oz potatoes,
  cut into 1 cm/½
  inch cubes
100 g/4 oz marrow or
  courgettes, peeled
  and cut into 1 cm/
  ½ inch cubes
275 g/10 oz cabbage,
  coarsely sliced
100 g/4 oz carrot,
  sliced
100 g/4 oz celery,
  sliced
2 corn on the cobs,
  cut into 2.5 cm/
  1 inch lengths
  (about 350 g/12 oz)
chopped parsley to
  garnish

AMERICAN

4¼ cups beef stock
4¼ cups water
1 can (8 oz) tomato
  sauce
¼ cup minced onion
1¼ teaspoons
  crushed thyme
  leaves
1 clove garlic, minced
1 teaspoon salt
8 oz shoulder or
  chuck boneless
  beef, cut into
  ½ inch cubes
½ teaspoon whole
  black peppercorns
4 whole cloves
8 oz potatoes, cut into
  ½ inch cubes
¾ cup peeled squash,
  cut into ½ inch
  cubes
4 cups coarsely sliced
  cabbage
¾ cup sliced carrot
¾ cup sliced celery
2 ears corn, cut into
  1 inch lengths
  (about ¾ lb)
chopped parsley for
  garnish

Place the beef stock, water, tomato sauce,
onion, thyme, garlic, salt and meat in a pan.
Add the black peppercorns and cloves, tied in
muslin (cheesecloth) if liked. Bring to the boil,
cover and simmer for 40 minutes.

Add the potatoes and marrow (squash).
Cover and simmer for 10 minutes. Add the
cabbage, carrot, celery and corn. Cover and
simmer for about 10 minutes until the meat and
vegetables are tender. Serve the soup sprinkled
with chopped parsley.
Cooking time: about 1 hour
Serves 6 to 8

Chicken and Cheese Soup

METRIC/IMPERIAL	AMERICAN
1 × 2.25 kg/5 lb boiling chicken	1 × 5 lb stewing chicken
1 onion, quartered	1 onion, quartered
2 carrots, sliced	2 carrots, sliced
2 teaspoons salt	2 teaspoons salt
4 peppercorns	4 peppercorns
bouquet garni	bouquet garni
2.75 litres/5 pints water	6 pints water
2 green peppers, cored, seeded and sliced	2 green peppers, seeded and sliced
1 onion, thinly sliced into rings	1 onion, thinly sliced into rings
1 × 425 g/14 oz can chick peas, drained	1 can (14 oz) chick peas, drained
¼ teaspoon ground black pepper	¼ teaspoon ground black pepper
225 g/8 oz cheese, cubed	8 oz cheese, cubed
1 avocado, peeled, stoned and sliced, to garnish	1 avocado, peeled, pitted and sliced, for garnish

Place the chicken in a large pan with the quartered onion, carrots, 1 teaspoon of the salt, the peppercorns and bouquet garni. Pour over the water to completely cover the chicken. Bring to the boil, then simmer for about 2 hours until cooked and tender. Remove the chicken and wrap in foil. Boil the cooking liquid for 15 minutes to reduce. Strain and reserve.

Rinse out the pan and add the strained, reduced cooking liquid. Bring to the boil and skim off any scum. Add the peppers and onion rings and simmer for 10 minutes. Add the chick peas and simmer for a further 5 minutes.

Cut the chicken meat into pieces and add to the pan. Stir in the remaining salt and the pepper and simmer for 5 minutes. Stir in the cheese. When the cheese has melted, serve the soup in individual bowls, garnished with the avocado.

Cooking time: about 2½ hours
Serves 6 to 8

Chilli Beef Chowder

METRIC/IMPERIAL	AMERICAN
40 g/1½ oz lard	3 tablespoons shortening
1 large onion, finely sliced	1 large onion, finely sliced
1 small clove garlic, crushed	1 small clove garlic, minced
225 g/8 oz minced beef	1 cup ground beef
2 tablespoons flour	2 tablespoons flour
2 teaspoons chilli powder	2 teaspoons chili powder
600 ml/1 pint beef stock	2½ cups beef stock
1 tablespoon tomato purée	1 tablespoon tomato paste
1 × 227 g/8 oz can tomatoes	1 can (8 oz) tomatoes
1 × 198 g/7 oz can red kidney beans, drained	1 can (7 oz) red kidney beans, drained
¼ teaspoon ground black pepper	¼ teaspoon ground black pepper

Melt the lard (shortening) in a pan, add the onion and garlic and fry for 5 minutes. Add the beef and fry for 10 minutes, stirring frequently. Sprinkle in the flour and chilli powder and cook for 1 minute. Stir in the stock and tomato purée (paste). Cover and simmer for 25 minutes, then add the tomatoes with their juice, beans and black pepper. Simmer for a further 10 minutes. Serve with tortillas (see page 40).
Cooking time: 50 minutes
Serves 4

Nachos

METRIC/IMPERIAL
about 150 ml/¼ pint
  Red Chilli Sauce
  (see page 40)
175 g/6 oz tortilla
  chips (see page 45)
100 g/4 oz cheese,
  grated
Garnish:
diced tomato
diced onion
soured cream or
  Guacamole
sliced green pepper

AMERICAN
about ⅔ cup Red Chili
  Sauce (see page 40)
6 oz tortilla chips (see
  page 45)
1 cup grated cheese
Garnish:
diced tomato
diced onion
sour cream or
  Guacamole
sliced green pepper

Put the sauce in a pan and heat through. Place
the tortilla chips on a flameproof plate. Spoon
over the sauce and sprinkle with the cheese.
Place under a preheated grill (broiler) and cook
for 2 to 3 minutes.

Garnish with tomato, onion, soured cream or
Guacamole, or slices of green pepper.
Cooking time: 5 minutes
Serves 2 to 4

Tuna Bean Appetizer

METRIC/IMPERIAL
2 eating apples, cored
  and chopped
1 tablespoon lemon
  juice
1 × 198 g/7 oz can
  tuna, drained and
  flaked
1 small onion, finely
  chopped
2 sticks celery, finely
  sliced
1 × 425 g/15 oz can
  red kidney beans,
  drained
¼ teaspoon ground
  black pepper
4 tablespoons oil and
  vinegar dressing

AMERICAN
2 apples, cored and
  chopped
1 tablespoon lemon
  juice
1 can (7 oz) tuna,
  drained and flaked
1 small onion, finely
  chopped
2 stalks celery, finely
  sliced
1 can (15 oz) red
  kidney beans,
  drained
¼ teaspoon ground
  black pepper
¼ cup oil and vinegar
  dressing

Coat the apple with the lemon juice to prevent
discoloration. Place in a bowl with the tuna,
onion, celery and beans. Add the black pepper
and dressing, toss well. Chill for 30 minutes.
Serves 4 to 6

Guacamole

METRIC/IMPERIAL
1 small hot green
  chilli
2 ripe avocados,
  peeled, halved and
  stoned
1 small onion, finely
  chopped
1 teaspoon chopped
  coriander leaves
2 teaspoons lime or
  lemon juice
1 large tomato,
  skinned, diced and
  seeded
salt
tortilla chips, to serve
  (see page 45)

AMERICAN
1 small hot green chili
2 ripe avocados,
  peeled, halved and
  pitted
1 small onion, finely
  chopped
1 teaspoon chopped
  coriander leaves
2 teaspoons lime or
  lemon juice
1 large tomato,
  peeled, diced and
  seeded
salt
tortilla chips, to serve
  (see page 45)

Pound the green chilli using a pestle and
mortar. Mash the avocado flesh lightly in a
bowl. Add the onion, ground chilli, coriander,
lime or lemon juice, tomato and salt to taste.
Mix thoroughly to make a fairly coarse-textured
mixture.

Serve as a dip with tortilla chips.
Serves 4

Guacamole

Cheese and Chilli Dip

METRIC/IMPERIAL
225 g/8 oz mature
    Cheddar cheese,
    cubed
250 ml/8 fl oz soured
    cream
2 green chillies,
    seeded and diced
½ clove garlic,
    crushed
¼ teaspoon salt
To serve:
carrot sticks
celery sticks
tortilla chips (see
    page 45)

AMERICAN
1 cup cubed sharp
    Cheddar cheese
1 cup sour cream
1 can (4 oz) diced
    green chilies
½ clove garlic,
    minced
¼ teaspoon salt
To serve:
carrot sticks
celery stalks
tortilla chips (see
    page 45)

Place the cheese and soured cream in a blender and blend until smooth. Transfer to a bowl and stir in the chillies, garlic and salt. Check the consistency, adding more soured cream if necessary. Chill until required.

Serve with the carrot, celery and tortilla chips for dipping.

Serves 4 to 6

Avocado with Prawns (Shrimp)

METRIC/IMPERIAL
2 avocados, halved
    and stoned
lemon juice
2 tablespoons
    mayonnaise
1 tablespoon tomato
    ketchup
1 tablespoon cream
1 teaspoon chilli
    sauce
¼ teaspoon garlic salt
100 g/4 oz peeled
    prawns
lime or lemon
    wedges to serve

AMERICAN
2 avocados, halved
    and pitted
lemon juice
2 tablespoons
    mayonnaise
1 tablespoon tomato
    ketchup
1 tablespoon cream
1 teaspoon chili sauce
¼ teaspoon garlic salt
⅔ cup shelled shrimp
lime or lemon
    wedges to serve

Rub the cut surface of the avocados with lemon juice to prevent discoloration. Mix the mayonnaise, tomato ketchup, cream, chilli sauce, salt and prawns (shrimp) together. Spoon into the avocados.

Serve with lemon or lime wedges.

Serves 4

Devilled Eggs

METRIC/IMPERIAL
6 hard-boiled eggs,
    cut in half
    lengthways
½ teaspoon salt
¼ teaspoon ground
    coriander
about 2 tablespoons
    mayonnaise
1 teaspoon finely
    chopped onion
2 green chillies, finely
    chopped

AMERICAN
6 hard-cooked eggs,
    cut in half
    lengthwise
½ teaspoon salt
¼ teaspoon ground
    coriander
1 tablespoon
    mayonnaise
1 teaspoon minced
    onion
1 can (4 oz) diced
    green chilies,
    drained

Carefully remove the yolks from the eggs, reserving the whites. Press the yolks through a fine sieve into a bowl. Stir in the salt, coriander, mayonnaise, onion and chillies. Spoon back into the egg whites. Cover and chill until required.

Serves 6

Chilli Pizza

METRIC/IMPERIAL
2 flour tortillas,
25-30 cm/10-12 inches
in diameter (see
page 40)
450 g/1 lb Mozzarella
cheese, grated
450 g/1 lb mild
cooked chorizo
sausage, chopped
50 g/2 oz onion, finely
chopped
2 tomatoes, diced
1 × 70 g/2¾ oz can
pimentos or chillies,
drained and sliced

AMERICAN
2 flour tortillas,
10-12 inches in
diameter (see
page 40)
4 cups grated
Monterey Jack
cheese
1 lb mild chorizo
sausage, cooked
and chopped
½ cup minced onion
2 tomatoes, diced
1 can (3½ oz) whole
jalapeno chilies,
sliced crosswise

Place the tortillas on a baking sheet. Sprinkle over the cheese. Cover with the sausage, onion and tomatoes. Add the strips of pimento or chilli in a criss-cross pattern. Cook in a preheated moderately hot oven (200°C/400°F, Gas Mark 6) for about 8 minutes until the cheese has melted.

Cut into 8 wedges to serve as a starter or 4 to serve as a snack.
Cooking time: 8 minutes
Serves 4

Spicy Sausage Dip

METRIC/IMPERIAL
1 medium-sized ripe
avocado
1 tablespoon lemon
juice
¼ teaspoon dry
mustard
1 teaspoon
Worcestershire
sauce
2 drops Tabasco
sauce
225 g/8 oz Continental
sausage, finely
chopped
25 g/1 oz onion, finely
chopped
1 medium tomato,
skinned and
chopped

AMERICAN
1 medium-size ripe
avocado
1 tablespoon lemon
juice
¼ teaspoon dry
mustard
1 teaspoon
Worcestershire
sauce
2 drops hot pepper
sauce
8 oz summer
sausage, finely
chopped
¼ cup finely chopped
onion
1 medium-size
tomato, peeled and
chopped

Halve and peel the avocado and remove and reserve the stone (seed). Mash the avocado with the lemon juice. Add the mustard, Worcestershire sauce and Tabasco (hot pepper) sauce and mix well. Fold in the sausage, onion and tomato. Place the avocado stone (seed) in the centre of the mixture and chill.

Remove the stone (seed) and serve as a dip with vegetable sticks and potato crisps (chips) to dip.
Serves 4

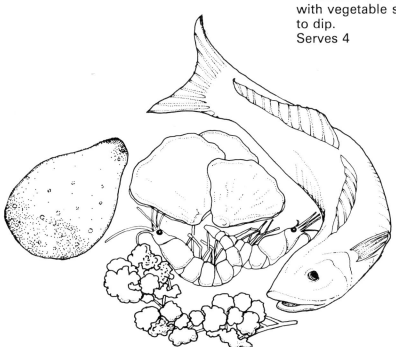

Fish Dishes

Shellfish Chilli Quiche

METRIC/IMPERIAL
Pastry:
100 g/4 oz plain flour
pinch of salt
25 g/1 oz lard
25 g/1 oz butter
1 tablespoon cold
water
Filling:
2 eggs
1 × 170 g/6 oz can
evaporated milk
2 tablespoons plain
flour
¾ teaspoon garlic salt
50 g/2 oz Cheddar
cheese, grated
50 g/2 oz Swiss
cheese, grated
50 g/2 oz onion,
chopped
1 × 100 g/4 oz can
chopped green
chillies or 2 fresh
green chillies,
seeded and
chopped
1 × 92 g/3¼ oz can
prawns, drained
Garnish:
parsley sprigs

AMERICAN
Dough:
1 cup all-purpose
flour
pinch of salt
2 tablespoons
shortening
2 tablespoons butter
1 tablespoon cold
water
Filling:
2 eggs
1 can (5 fl oz)
evaporated milk
2 tablespoons
all-purpose flour
¾ teaspoon garlic salt
½ cup grated
Cheddar cheese
½ cup grated
Monterey Jack
cheese
½ cup chopped onion
1 can (4 oz) chopped
green chilies
1 can (4½ oz)
medium shrimp,
drained
Garnish:
parsley sprigs

Sift the flour and salt into a bowl. Rub (cut) in the lard (shortening) and butter until the mixture resembles fine breadcrumbs. Add the water and mix in with a knife, then knead the dough together. Form into a smooth ball and turn onto a floured surface. Roll out the dough and use to line a 20 cm (8 inch) flan tin or dish (quiche pan). Prick the bottom with a fork and place on a baking sheet. Cook in a preheated hot oven (230°C/450°F, Gas Mark 8) for 6 minutes. Remove from the oven. Reduce the oven temperature to 180°C/350°F, Gas Mark 4.

Beat the eggs, evaporated milk, flour and garlic salt together (the mixture need not be smooth). Stir in the cheeses, onion and green chillies. Pour into the pastry case (pie shell). Reserve 6 prawns (shrimp) and sprinkle rest on top of the custard mixture. Cook in the preheated oven for about 35 to 40 minutes until a knife inserted in the centre comes out clean.

Leave to cool for 15 minutes before serving. Garnish with the reserved prawns (shrimp) and parsley.
Cooking time: about 50 minutes
Serves 6

Shellfish Chilli Quiche
(Photograph: Old El Paso Products)

Marinated Raw Fish

METRIC/IMPERIAL	AMERICAN
450 g/1 lb mixed fish, including prawns or scallops and white fish such as haddock, plaice, sole	1 lb mixed fish, including shrimp or bay scallops, and white fish such as haddock, pompano, sole
350 ml/12 fl oz lime or lemon juice	1½ cups lime or lemon juice
2 canned jalapeno chillies, or 1-2 red chillies or pimentos, finely chopped	2 canned jalapeno chilies, or 1-2 red chilies or pimientos, finely chopped
1 onion, coarsely chopped	1 onion, coarsely chopped
1 large tomato, skinned, seeded and coarsely chopped	1 large tomato, peeled, seeded and coarsely chopped
6 tablespoons olive oil	6 tablespoons olive oil
2 tablespoons wine vinegar	2 tablespoons wine vinegar
¼ teaspoon dried oregano	¼ teaspoon dried oregano
1 teaspoon freshly ground black pepper	1 teaspoon freshly ground black pepper
salt	salt
6 lettuce leaves, chilled	6 lettuce leaves, chilled
1-2 limes, cut into wedges, to garnish	1-2 limes, cut into wedges, for garnish

Clean and rinse the fish thoroughly in cold water; pat dry with kitchen paper towels. Shell and de-vein the prawns (shrimp) and scallops and leave them whole. Skin, bone and shred the white fish.

Place all the fish in a glass or ceramic bowl and pour over the lime or lemon juice. Cover and refrigerate for 4 hours, turning occasionally with a wooden spoon. Drain off the juice.

Combine the chillies, onion, tomato, oil, vinegar, oregano and pepper with salt to taste. Add to the fish and mix well. Refrigerate for 2 to 3 hours. Leave to stand at room temperature for 15 minutes before serving.

Line cocktail glasses or salad plates with lettuce, arrange the fish on top and garnish with lime wedges.

Serves 6

Fish Yucatan Style

METRIC/IMPERIAL	AMERICAN
1 large or 2 small red snapper, plaice or haddock, weighing about 2.25 kg/5 lb, cleaned	1 red snapper, pompano or haddock, weighing about 5 lb, cleaned
2 tablespoons lime juice	2 tablespoons lime juice
1 tablespoon salt	1 tablespoon salt
1 teaspoon freshly ground black pepper	1 teaspoon freshly ground black pepper
3 tablespoons olive oil	3 tablespoons olive oil
1 small onion, finely chopped	1 small onion, finely chopped
1 green pepper, cored, seeded and coarsely chopped	1 green pepper, seeded and coarsely chopped
175 g/6 oz pumpkin seeds, chopped (optional)	1 cup pumpkin seeds, chopped (optional)
2 tablespoons chopped coriander leaves	2 tablespoons chopped coriander leaves
120 ml/4 fl oz unsweetened orange juice	½ cup unsweetened orange juice
2 hard-boiled eggs, sliced (optional)	2 hard-cooked eggs, sliced (optional)
2 limes, cut into wedges (optional)	2 limes, cut into wedges (optional)

Rinse and dry the fish; rub all over with lime juice. Place in an ovenproof dish and sprinkle with the salt and pepper. Heat the oil in a frying pan, add the onion, green pepper, pumpkin seeds, if using, and half of the coriander leaves and fry until the vegetables are soft but not brown. Spread this mixture on top of the fish and pour over the orange juice.

Cover and cook in a preheated moderate oven (180°C/350°F, Gas Mark 4) for 25 to 30 minutes or until the fish flakes easily when tested with a fork at the thickest part.

Garnish with the sliced eggs and lime wedges, if using, before serving.

Cooking time: about 35 minutes

Serves 6

Seafood Enchilada Casserole

METRIC/IMPERIAL	AMERICAN
1 × 350 g/12 oz can tuna chunks, drained	1 can (12½ oz) tuna chunks, drained
225 g/8 oz Cheddar cheese, grated	2 cups grated Monterey Jack cheese
1 tablespoon oil	1 tablespoon oil
1 large onion, chopped	1 large onion, chopped
1 clove garlic, crushed	1 clove garlic, minced
1 × 397 g/14 oz can tomatoes	1 can (14½ oz) tomatoes
1 × 225 g/8 oz can tomato sauce	1 can (8 oz) tomato sauce
50 g/2 oz tomato purée	¼ cup tomato paste
1 green chilli, diced	¼ cup diced green chilies
1 teaspoon ground cumin	1 teaspoon ground cumin
1 teaspoon crumbled oregano	1 teaspoon crumbled oregano
1 teaspoon sugar	1 teaspoon sugar
½ teaspoon salt	½ teaspoon salt
8 corn tortillas, warmed (see page 40)	8 corn tortillas, warmed (see page 40)

Combine the tuna with half of the cheese. Heat the oil in a pan, add the onion and garlic and fry until the onion is soft. Stir in the tomatoes with their juice, tomato sauce, tomato purée (paste), chilli, cumin, oregano, sugar and salt. Simmer for 15 minutes.

Spoon 120 ml/4 fl oz (½ cup) of the sauce in the bottom of a shallow casserole. Spoon equal amounts of the tuna mixture on to each tortilla. Roll up and place, seam side down, in the casserole. Pour the remaining sauce over the enchiladas. Top with the remaining cheese.

Cook in a preheated moderately hot oven (190°C/375°F, Gas Mark 5) for 20 to 25 minutes.
Cooking time: 40 to 45 minutes
Serves 4

Hot Chilli Fish Curry

METRIC/IMPERIAL	AMERICAN
25 g/1 oz butter	2 tablespoons butter
1 tablespoon curry powder	1 tablespoon curry powder
about 1 teaspoon chilli powder	about 1 teaspoon chili powder
2 onions, chopped	2 onions, chopped
1 clove garlic, crushed	1 clove garlic, minced
600 ml/1 pint chicken stock	2½ cups chicken stock or broth
2 tablespoons tomato purée	2 tablespoons tomato paste
juice of 1 lemon	juice of 1 lemon
2 teaspoons honey	2 teaspoons honey
450 g/1 lb cooked white fish fillets, diced, or 225 g/8 oz peeled prawns	1 lb cooked white fish fillets, diced, or 1⅓ cups shelled shrimp
about ¼ teaspoon salt	about ¼ teaspoon salt

Melt the butter in a pan, add the curry and chilli powders and cook over a low heat for 1 minute. Add the onions and garlic and fry for 3 minutes. Stir in the stock, tomato purée (paste), lemon juice and honey. Cover and simmer for 1 hour. The sauce should be quite thick.

Stir in the fish and cook for a further 10 minutes; if using prawns (shrimp), cook for 5 minutes only. Taste and add salt. Serve with rice.
Cooking time: about 1¼ hours
Serves 4

Tortilla Tuna Casserole

METRIC/IMPERIAL	AMERICAN
1 tablespoon oil	1 tablespoon oil
1 medium onion, chopped	1 medium-size onion, chopped
1 clove garlic, crushed	1 clove garlic, minced
1 × 425 g/15 oz can tomato sauce	1 can (15 oz) tomato sauce
150 g/5 oz stoned black olives, sliced	1 cup pitted and sliced ripe olives
1 green chilli, diced	¼ cup diced green chilies
1 teaspoon ground cumin	1 teaspoon ground cumin
1 teaspoon sugar	1 teaspoon sugar
½ teaspoon salt	½ teaspoon salt
1 × 198 g/7 oz can tuna chunks, drained	1 can (6½ oz) tuna chunks, drained
225 g/8 oz Cheddar cheese, grated	2 cups grated Monterey Jack cheese
225 g/8 oz cottage cheese	1 cup cottage cheese
1 egg	1 egg
4 corn tortillas (see page 40)	4 corn tortillas (see page 40)

Heat the oil in a pan, add the onion and garlic and fry until the onion is soft. Stir in the tomato sauce, olives, chilli, cumin, sugar and salt. Cover and simmer for 15 minutes. Remove from the heat. Stir in the tuna.

Spoon half the mixture into a shallow casserole. Top with half the cheese. Mix the cottage cheese and egg together. Spoon over the cheese. Place the tortillas over the cottage cheese mixture. Mound the remaining tuna mixture over the top and sprinkle with the remaining cheese.

Cook in a preheated moderate oven (180°C/350°F, Gas Mark 4) for 30 minutes. Leave to cool for 10 minutes before serving.
Cooking time: 50 minutes
Serves 4 to 6

Taco Oysters

METRIC/IMPERIAL	AMERICAN
rock or sea salt	rock salt
36 uncooked oysters on the half shell	3 dozen raw oysters on the half shell
1 × 425 g/15 oz can tomato sauce	1 can (15 oz) tomato sauce
3 tablespoons lemon juice	3 tablespoons lemon juice
1 tablespoon sugar	1 tablespoon sugar
¾ teaspoon salt	¾ teaspoon salt
½ teaspoon ground black pepper	½ teaspoon ground black pepper
½ teaspoon Tabasco sauce	½ teaspoon hot pepper sauce
18 rashers streaky bacon, cut crossways into 4 pieces, partly fried	18 bacon slices, cut crosswise into 4 pieces, partially fried
100 g/4 oz mature Cheddar cheese, finely grated	1 cup finely grated sharp Cheddar cheese

Sprinkle a little salt in the bottom of a shallow ovenproof dish. Arrange the oysters in the dish. Mix the tomato sauce, lemon juice, sugar, salt, pepper and Tabasco (hot pepper) sauce together. Spoon an equal amount of tomato mixture over the oysters. Top each oyster with 2 pieces of bacon. Sprinkle with the cheese.

Cook in a preheated hot oven (230°C/450°F, Gas Mark 8) for 7 to 8 minutes or until the oysters are cooked and the edges curl.
Cooking time: 7 to 8 minutes
Serves 6

Taco Oysters
(Photograph: US National Marine Fisheries Service)

Red Snapper in Coriander

METRIC/IMPERIAL	AMERICAN
1 kg/2 lb red snapper, bream or other white fish fillets	2 lb red snapper or other saltwater fish fillets
4 tablespoons lime or lemon juice	¼ cup lime or lemon juice
2 teaspoons salt	2 teaspoons salt
4 tablespoons olive oil	¼ cup olive oil
25 g/1 oz fresh breadcrumbs	½ cup soft bread crumbs
1 clove garlic, crushed	1 clove garlic, minced
6 tablespoons crushed coriander leaves	6 tablespoons crushed coriander leaves
1 teaspoon grated lime or lemon rind	1 teaspoon grated lime or lemon rind
freshly ground black pepper	freshly ground black pepper

Lightly oil a heavy frying pan. Rub the fish with half of the lime or lemon juice and 1 teaspoon of the salt and place in the pan, skin side down. Add water to cover. Simmer the fish gently for 5 minutes, turning twice.

In another pan, heat half of the oil, then add the breadcrumbs, garlic, remaining salt and 4 tablespoons of the coriander. Cook over a low heat, stirring constantly until the crumbs are browned. Spread over the fish. Simmer for 7 to 10 minutes or until the fish flakes easily when tested with a fork.

Mix the remaining lime or lemon juice and oil together and pour over the fish. Cook for 2 to 3 minutes. Combine the remaining coriander and grated lime or lemon rind and sprinkle over the fish. Season with pepper to taste.
Cooking time: about 20 minutes
Serves 4 to 6

Baked Spiced Fish

METRIC/IMPERIAL	AMERICAN
¼ green pepper, cored, seeded and chopped	¼ green pepper, seeded and chopped
bunch of coriander leaves, chopped	bunch of coriander leaves, chopped
1 teaspoon ground cumin	1 teaspoon ground cumin
½ teaspoon chilli powder	½ teaspoon chili powder
½ teaspoon garlic salt	½ teaspoon garlic salt
1 tablespoon garlic vinegar or 1 tablespoon wine vinegar with ½ clove garlic, crushed	1 tablespoon garlic vinegar or 1 tablespoon wine vinegar with ½ clove garlic, minced
450 g-1 kg/1-2 lb whole white fish, cleaned	1-2 lb whole white fish, cleaned
25 g/1 oz butter	2 tablespoons butter

Mix the green pepper, coriander leaves, cumin, chilli powder, salt and vinegar together. Stuff the fish with the mixture, rubbing a little on the outside of the fish as well. Dot the fish with butter and, if necessary, secure with thread or wooden cocktail sticks (toothpicks), or wrap in foil. Put in a greased ovenproof dish.

Cook in a preheated moderate oven (180°C/350°F, Gas Mark 4) for about 25 minutes, depending on size, until the flesh flakes easily. If baking uncovered, baste with the butter and turn the fish over halfway through cooking. When the fish is cooked, transfer to a warm serving dish. If liked, thicken the cooking juices with a little cornflour (cornstarch) and water mixture and cook for 1 minute, stirring. Serve as a sauce with the fish.
Cooking time: about 25 minutes
Serves 4 to 6

Tuna Tortilla Rolls

METRIC/IMPERIAL	AMERICAN
1 × 198 g/7 oz can tuna chunks, drained	1 can (6½ oz) tuna chunks, drained
50 g/2 oz Cheddar cheese, grated	½ cup grated Monterey Jack cheese
25 g/1 oz celery, sliced	¼ cup sliced celery
1 small tomato, seeded and chopped	¼ cup seeded, chopped tomato
4 tablespoons mayonnaise	¼ cup mayonnaise
2 tablespoons diced green chillies	2 tablespoons diced green chilies
1 tablespoon chopped onion	1 tablespoon chopped onion
½ teaspoon crumbled oregano	½ teaspoon crumbled oregano
4 corn tortillas, warmed (see page 40)	4 corn tortillas, warmed (see page 40)

Combine the tuna with the cheese, celery, tomato, mayonnaise, chillies, onion and oregano.

Spoon the mixture equally on to the tortillas. Roll up the tortillas to secure the mixture. Serve with salad.

Serves 2 to 4

Coriander Grilled (Broiled) Fish

METRIC/IMPERIAL	AMERICAN
450 g/1 lb white fish steaks or cutlets	1 lb white fish steaks or cutlets
salt	salt
bunch of coriander leaves, finely chopped	bunch of coriander leaves, finely chopped
½ green pepper, cored, seeded and finely chopped	½ green pepper, seeded and finely chopped
¼ teaspoon garlic salt	¼ teaspoon garlic salt
juice of ½ lemon	juice of ½ lemon
25 g/1 oz butter	2 tablespoons butter
Garnish:	**Garnish:**
lemon slices	lemon slices
parsley sprig	parsley sprig

Rub the fish with a little salt. Mix the chopped coriander leaves, green pepper, garlic salt and lemon juice together. Smear the fish with this mixture. Dot with half the butter.

Place the fish under a preheated medium grill (broiler) and cook for about 5 minutes on each side, using the remaining butter to dot the second side.

When cooked, remove the fish to a heated serving dish and pour the pan juices over. Garnish the fish with the lemon slices and parsley sprig.

Cooking time: about 10 minutes

Serves 4

Veracruz Bream

METRIC/IMPERIAL	AMERICAN
750 g/1½ lb canned tomatoes	1½ lb canned tomatoes
4 tablespoons oil	¼ cup oil
2 onions, chopped	2 onions, chopped
1 clove garlic, crushed	1 clove garlic, minced
2 small, dried, hot red chillies, or canned jalapeno chillies, chopped	2 small, dried, hot red chilies or jalapeno chilies, chopped
8 stuffed green olives, chopped	8 stuffed green olives, chopped
4 stoned black olives, chopped	4 pitted ripe olives, chopped
750 g/1½ lb sea bream or red snapper fillets	1½ lb sea bream or red snapper fillets
40 g/1½ oz plain flour, seasoned with salt and pepper	3 tablespoons all-purpose flour, seasoned with salt and pepper
50 g/2 oz butter	¼ cup butter

Place the tomatoes and their juice in a blender and blend until puréed. Heat the oil in a large pan, add the onions and garlic and fry until soft. Stir in the puréed tomato with the chillies and olives. Simmer the sauce for 20 minutes.

Meanwhile coat the fish in the seasoned flour. Melt the butter in a large frying pan, add the fish and fry for about 5 minutes on each side until cooked. Transfer to a heated serving dish and pour over the sauce.

Cooking time: 35 minutes

Serves 4

Meat & Poultry Dishes

Chilli Heroes

METRIC/IMPERIAL	AMERICAN
1 medium onion, finely chopped	2 tablespoons instant minced onion
1 clove garlic, chopped	½ teaspoon instant minced garlic
2 tablespoons oil	2 tablespoons oil
450 g/1 lb minced beef	1 lb ground beef
1 × 397 g/14 oz can tomatoes, broken up	1 can (1 lb) tomatoes, broken up
2 teaspoons chilli powder	2 teaspoons chili powder
1 teaspoon salt	1 teaspoon salt
½ teaspoon crumbled oregano leaves	½ teaspoon crumbled oregano leaves
black pepper	black pepper
40 g/1½ oz stoned olives, sliced	¼ cup pitted sliced olives
1 crusty loaf bread, about 30 cm/ 12 inches long	1 lb Italian bread, 12 inches long
1 avocado	1 avocado
1 large tomato, diced	1 large tomato, diced

If using instant onion and garlic, rehydrate in water for 10 minutes. Heat the oil in a large frying pan, add the onion and garlic and fry for 5 minutes. Add the beef, cook and stir for about 5 minutes until brown. Pour off any excess fat. Stir in the tomatoes, chilli powder, salt, oregano and pepper to taste. Bring to the boil and simmer, uncovered, for 10 minutes. Stir in the olives.

Put the bread on a baking sheet. Place in a preheated moderate oven (180°C/350°F, Gas Mark 4) until hot. Split in half lengthways and slightly hollow out the centres. Fill with the hot beef mixture. Cut each length in half crossways and garnish with avocado slices and tomato.
Cooking time: 25 to 30 minutes
Serves 4

Sombrero Beef Strips

METRIC/IMPERIAL	AMERICAN
1 kg/2 lb steak, cut 2 cm/¾ inch thick	2 lb beef round steak, cut ¾ inch thick
3 tablespoons oil	3 tablespoons oil
1 × 225 g/8 oz can tomato sauce	1 can (8 oz) tomato sauce
1 × 340 g/12 oz can sweetcorn kernels	1 can (16 oz) whole kernel corn
1 onion, thinly sliced	1 onion, thinly sliced
4 tablespoons water	¼ cup water
2 teaspoons chilli powder	2 teaspoons chili powder
1 teaspoon ground coriander	1 teaspoon ground coriander
1 teaspoon salt	1 teaspoon salt
1 medium green pepper, cored, seeded and cut into 2.5 cm/1 inch pieces	1 medium-size green pepper, seeded and cut into 1 inch pieces
5 tablespoons chilli sauce	⅓ cup chili sauce
100 g/4 oz Cheddar cheese, grated	1 cup grated Monterey Jack cheese

Slice the beef into strips 3 mm/⅛ inch thick and 7.5-10 cm/3-4 inches in length. (If possible, partially freeze the beef so that it can be cut easily into the very thin strips.)

Heat the oil in a pan, add the beef strips and fry until brown. Pour off any excess fat. Add the tomato sauce, drained corn, onion, water, chilli powder, coriander and salt and mix thoroughly. Turn into a shallow casserole.

Cover and cook in a preheated moderate oven (180°C/350°F, Gas Mark 4) for about 45 minutes. Stir in the green pepper, top with the chilli sauce and sprinkle with the cheese. Continue cooking for 15 minutes.
Cooking time: 1 to 1¼ hours
Serves 6 to 8

Chilli Heroes
(Photograph: American Spice Trade Association)

Coastal Style Pork

METRIC/IMPERIAL	AMERICAN
50 g/2 oz lard	¼ cup shortening
1.5 kg/3 lb lean boneless pork, cut into 4 cm/1½ inch cubes	3 lb lean boneless pork, cut into 1½ inch cubes
1 tablespoon sugar	1 tablespoon sugar
3 tablespoons plain flour	3 tablespoons all-purpose flour
salt and freshly ground pepper	salt and freshly ground pepper
2 onions, chopped	2 onions, chopped
450-750 ml/¾-1¼ pints beef stock	2-3 cups beef stock
1 teaspoon coriander seeds, soaked in 2 tablespoons warm water	1 teaspoon coriander seeds, soaked in 2 tablespoons warm water
1 clove garlic, chopped	1 clove garlic, chopped
1 teaspoon crushed dried chilli	1 teaspoon crushed chili chipotle (or other chili)
2 tomatoes, skinned, seeded and coarsely chopped	2 tomatoes, peeled, seeded and coarsely chopped
225 g/8 oz peeled and cored fresh pineapple, coarsely chopped	1 cup peeled, cored and coarsely chopped fresh pineapple
2 medium yams or sweet potatoes, peeled and diced	2 medium yams or sweet potatoes, peeled and diced

Melt the lard (shortening) in a heavy frying pan, add the pork and fry, turning frequently, until brown on all sides. Transfer to a large flameproof casserole, using a slotted spoon. Sprinkle with the sugar and cook, stirring constantly, over a very low heat for 3 to 5 minutes or until the sugar dissolves completely. Add the flour, salt and pepper to taste and cook, stirring, for 5 minutes. Remove from the heat.

Add the onions to the fat remaining in the frying pan and fry until transparent and soft but not brown. Add the stock, stirring well to scrape up any sediment from the bottom of the pan, and bring to the boil. Lower the heat.

Strain the liquor from the coriander seeds and mix the liquor with the garlic and crushed chilli, then add to the pan. Add the tomatoes and cook for 5 minutes, stirring. Pour this mixture over the pork cubes and bring to the boil. Cover and cook the pork in a preheated moderate oven (180°C/350°F, Gas Mark 4) for about 1½ to 2 hours or until tender.

Using a slotted spoon, remove the meat and set aside. Strain the gravy into a large container and skim off excess fat. Return the meat to the casserole and add the gravy with the pineapple and yams or sweet potatoes. Return to the oven for 20 to 25 minutes until the fruit and vegetables are tender.
Cooking time: 2½ to 3 hours
Serves 6

Chilli con Carne

METRIC/IMPERIAL	AMERICAN
2 tablespoons oil	2 tablespoons oil
1 onion, sliced	1 onion, sliced
1 clove garlic, crushed	1 clove garlic, minced
1 red pepper, cored, seeded and sliced	1 red pepper, seeded and sliced
1 dried hot red chilli, crumbled	1 dried hot red chili, crumbled, or 1 canned Jalapeno chili, chopped
1 kg/2 lb braising steak, cubed	2 lb chuck steak, cubed
450 ml/¾ pint Red Chilli Sauce (see page 40)	2 cups Red Chili Sauce (see page 40)
1 × 425 g/15 oz can red kidney beans, drained	1 can (14 oz) red kidney beans, drained
25 g/1 oz brown sugar	2 tablespoons brown sugar
¼ teaspoon salt	¼ teaspoon salt
¼ teaspoon ground black pepper	¼ teaspoon ground black pepper
1 tablespoon finely chopped coriander	1 tablespoon finely chopped coriander

Heat the oil in a pan, add the onion, garlic and red pepper and fry until soft. Add the chilli and beef and fry until the meat is brown on all sides. Stir in the sauce, beans, sugar, salt and pepper.

Cover and simmer for 2 hours until the meat is tender. Stir in the coriander just before serving.
Cooking time: 2¼ hours
Serves 6

Mexican Pork and Rice

METRIC/IMPERIAL	AMERICAN
2 tablespoons oil	2 tablespoons oil
2 onions, chopped	2 onions, chopped
450 g/1 lb minced pork	1 lb ground pork
225 g/8 oz sausage meat	1 cup sausage meat
1 green pepper, cored, seeded and sliced	1 green pepper, seeded and sliced
75 g/3 oz raisins	½ cup raisins
1 clove garlic, crushed	1 clove garlic, minced
½ teaspoon ground cumin	½ teaspoon ground cumin
½ teaspoon ground coriander	½ teaspoon ground coriander
1 small, dried, hot red chilli, crumbled	1 small, dried, hot red chili, crumbled
¼ teaspoon salt	¼ teaspoon salt
¼ teaspoon ground black pepper	¼ teaspoon ground black pepper
175 g/6 oz long grain rice, soaked in cold water for 30 minutes	1 cup long grain rice, soaked in cold water for 30 minutes
1 × 397 g/14 oz can tomatoes	1 can (14 oz) tomatoes
120 ml/4 fl oz water	½ cup water
2 tablespoons tomato purée	2 tablespoons tomato paste
2 tablespoons lemon juice	2 tablespoons lemon juice
3 tablespoons pine nuts or peanuts	3 tablespoons pine nuts or peanuts

Heat the oil in a flameproof casserole, add the onions and fry until soft. Stir in the pork and sausage meat and fry until they change colour. Stir in the green pepper, raisins, garlic, cumin, coriander, chilli, salt, pepper and drained rice. Fry for 5 minutes, stirring. Add the tomatoes with their juice, water and tomato purée (paste) and bring to the boil. Cover and simmer for 10 minutes.

Place the casserole in a preheated moderate oven (180°C/350°F, Gas Mark 4) and cook for 25 minutes. Remove from the oven and sprinkle the lemon juice and nuts over. Return to the oven and cook, uncovered, for a further 10 minutes.
Cooking time: about 1 hour
Serves 4 to 6

Beef-Stuffed Peppers

METRIC/IMPERIAL	AMERICAN
450 g/1 lb minced beef	1 lb ground beef
1 onion, chopped	1 onion, chopped
1 × 298 g/10½ oz can condensed tomato soup	1 can (10¾ oz) condensed tomato soup
100 g/4 oz peeled and diced pear	1 cup peeled, diced pears
40 g/1½ oz raisins	¼ cup raisins
1 medium clove garlic, crushed	1 medium-size clove garlic, minced
¼ teaspoon ground cinnamon	¼ teaspoon ground cinnamon
6 medium green peppers	6 medium-size green peppers
Soured cream and nut sauce:	**Sour cream and nut sauce:**
120 ml/4 fl oz soured cream	½ cup sour cream
25 g/1 oz blanched almonds, finely chopped	¼ cup finely chopped almonds
2 tablespoons milk	2 tablespoons milk
good pinch of ground cinnamon	generous pinch of ground cinnamon

Place the beef and onion in a frying pan and cook until the beef is brown and the onion is soft, breaking the meat up as it cooks. Pour off any excess fat. Stir in the tomato soup, pears, raisins, garlic and cinnamon. Cover and simmer for 10 minutes.

Meanwhile, remove the cores and seeds from the peppers. Cook in boiling salted water for 5 minutes; drain. Spoon the filling into the peppers and arrange in a shallow ovenproof dish. Cook in a preheated moderate oven (180°C/350°F, Gas Mark 4) for about 25 minutes.

Meanwhile make the sauce: combine the soured cream, almonds, milk and cinnamon and chill. Serve the stuffed peppers with the sauce.
Cooking time: about 45 minutes
Serves 6

Tamale Beef Pie

METRIC/IMPERIAL	AMERICAN
1 kg/2 lb minced beef	2 lb ground beef
1 large green pepper, cored, seeded and cut into strips	1 large green pepper, seeded and cut into strips
1 medium onion, chopped	1 medium-size onion, chopped
1 × 397 g/14 oz can tomatoes	1 can (16 oz) tomatoes
1 × 225 g/8 oz can tomato sauce	1 can (8 oz) tomato sauce
1-2 tablespoons chilli powder	1-2 tablespoons chili powder
1 tablespoon sugar	1 tablespoon sugar
1 teaspoon salt	1 teaspoon salt
1 clove garlic, crushed	1 clove garlic, minced
100 g/4 oz Cheddar cheese, grated	1 cup grated Monterey Jack cheese
75 g/3 oz stoned black olives, sliced	½ cup sliced pitted ripe olives
180 g/6¼ oz cornmeal	1¼ cups enriched cornmeal
15 g/½ oz plain flour	2 tablespoons all-purpose flour
2 tablespoons sugar	2 tablespoons sugar
1 tablespoon baking powder	1 tablespoon baking powder
½ teaspoon salt	½ teaspoon salt
150 ml/¼ pint milk	⅔ cup milk
1 egg	1 egg
25 g/1 oz lard, melted	2 tablespoons melted shortening

Place the beef, green pepper and onion in a large frying pan and fry until lightly browned, breaking up the meat as it cooks. Pour off any excess fat. Add the tomatoes with their juice, tomato sauce, chilli powder, sugar, salt and garlic. Simmer for 25 to 30 minutes, stirring occasionally. Stir in the cheese and olives. Transfer to a casserole, levelling the top.

Meanwhile sift the cornmeal, flour, sugar, baking powder and salt together. Stir in the milk, egg and lard (shortening). Pour over the surface of the hot meat mixture. Cook in a preheated hot oven (220°C/425°F, Gas Mark 7) for 15 to 20 minutes until the topping is cooked.
Cooking time: about 1 hour
Serves 6

Empanadas

METRIC/IMPERIAL	AMERICAN
1 tablespoon oil	1 tablespoon oil
1 small onion, chopped	1 small onion, chopped
225 g/8 oz minced beef	1 cup ground beef
2 tomatoes, chopped	2 tomatoes, chopped
2 tablespoons raisins	2 tablespoons raisins
2 tablespoons stoned and chopped green olives	2 tablespoons pitted and chopped green olives
2 teaspoons chilli powder	2 teaspoons chili powder
¼ teaspoon salt	¼ teaspoon salt
½ teaspoon paprika	½ teaspoon paprika
1 teaspoon crushed oregano leaves	1 teaspoon crushed oregano leaves
2 hard-boiled eggs, chopped	2 hard-cooked eggs, chopped
225 g/8 oz shortcrust pastry	½ lb pie dough
beaten egg to glaze (optional)	beaten egg for glaze (optional)

Heat the oil in a frying pan, add the onion and beef and fry for 10 minutes until brown. Pour off any excess fat. Stir in the tomatoes, raisins, olives, chilli powder, salt, paprika and oregano. Cook for 10 minutes, stirring occasionally. Remove from the heat and stir in the eggs. Leave to cool.

Divide the dough into 4 pieces. Roll out each piece on a lightly floured board to a 15 cm/ 6 inch circle, 3mm/⅛ inch thick. Spoon a quarter of the meat mixture on to one side of each circle and moisten the edges with water. Fold the pastry over the filling to form a semi-circle. Moisten the edges and press to seal, then crimp. Prick the tops of the empanadas to allow steam to escape. If used, brush the tops with beaten egg. Put on a baking sheet. Cook in a preheated moderately hot oven (200°C/400°F, Gas Mark 6) for 30 minutes or until golden. Serve hot.
Cooking time: 50 minutes
Makes 4
Note: to serve empanadas as appetizers, make them smaller. Roll out the pastry and cut out 7.5 cm/3 inch circles, adding less filling and cooking for about 20 minutes. Other fillings may be used, Picadillo (see page 28) is a good choice.

Empanadas
(Photograph: American Spice Trade
Association)

Meatball Chilli

METRIC/IMPERIAL	AMERICAN
450 g/1 lb dried black-eyed peas	1 lb dried black-eyed peas
1.5 litres/2½ pints water	6 cups water
2¼ teaspoons salt	2¼ teaspoons salt
1-1.25 kg/2-2½ lb minced beef	2-2½ lb ground beef
25 g/1 oz tortilla chips, crushed (page 45)	½ cup crushed tortilla chips (see page 45)
1 onion, chopped	1 onion, chopped
1 egg	1 egg
1 × 425 g/15 oz can tomato sauce	1 can (15 oz) tomato sauce
1 × 397 g/14 oz tomatoes	1 can (16 oz) tomatoes
120 ml/4 fl oz water	½ cup water
1-2 tablespoons chilli powder	1-2 tablespoons chili powder
½ teaspoon dried basil	½ teaspoon dried basil
1 clove garlic, crushed	1 clove garlic, minced
2 medium green peppers, cored, seeded and cut into 1 cm/½ inch pieces	2 medium-size green peppers, seeded and cut into ½ inch pieces
15 g/½ oz plain flour	2 tablespoons all-purpose flour
25 g/1 oz lard	2 tablespoons lard

Place the peas in a pan, add the water and 1 teaspoon of the salt; bring to the boil and cook for 10 minutes. Cover, remove from the heat and leave to stand for 1 hour. Return to the heat, cover and simmer for 1 hour until tender.

Meanwhile mix together the beef, crushed tortilla chips, onion, egg and 1 teaspoon of the salt. Mix in 120 ml/4 fl oz/½ cup of the tomato sauce. Form the mixture into balls, using approximately 50 g/2 oz/¼ cup of the meat for each one. Chill the meatballs.

Combine the remaining tomato sauce with the tomatoes and their juice, water, chilli powder, basil, remaining salt and garlic in a large pan. Simmer for 30 minutes, stirring.

Drain the peas, reserving the liquid. Add the peas, 350 ml/12 fl oz/1½ cups of the reserved liquid and the green peppers to the tomato mixture. Dredge the meatballs in flour. Melt the lard in a pan, add the meatballs and fry until brown on all sides. Add the meatballs to the pea mixture, cover tightly and simmer for 30 minutes or until the meatballs are cooked and peas tender. Serve with crushed tortilla chips.

Cooking time: about 2½ hours
Serves 8

Picadillo

METRIC/IMPERIAL	AMERICAN
75 g/3 oz lard or bacon fat	6 tablespoons shortening or bacon fat
750 g/1½ lb minced beef	1½ lb ground beef
1 large onion, finely chopped	1½ cups finely chopped onion
4 tablespoons red wine or dry sherry	¼ cup red wine or pale dry sherry
3 tablespoons lime or lemon juice	3 tablespoons lime or lemon juice
2 tomatoes, skinned and chopped	2 tomatoes, peeled and chopped
2 small hot green chillies, chopped	2 small hot green chilies, chopped
75 g/3 oz stuffed green olives, sliced	½ cup stuffed green olives, sliced
3 tablespoons capers	3 tablespoons capers
75 g/3 oz raisins	½ cup raisins
2 large potatoes, cut into small cubes	2 large potatoes, cut into small cubes
1 clove garlic, crushed	1 clove garlic, minced
½ teaspoon ground cumin	½ teaspoon ground cumin
salt (optional)	salt (optional)
50 g/2 oz blanched almonds, chopped and toasted, to garnish	½ cup chopped almonds, toasted, for garnish

Heat half of the lard (shortening) or bacon fat in a heavy frying pan, add the beef and onion and fry over a high heat, stirring constantly, until evenly browned. Lower the heat and add the wine or sherry and lime or lemon juice. Cook for 5 minutes. Stir in the tomatoes, chillies, olives, capers and raisins. Cover and simmer for 20 minutes.

Heat the remaining fat in another pan, add the potatoes, garlic and cumin and fry, turning, until evenly browned. Lower the heat and cook for 10 to 12 minutes or until the potatoes are tender.

Add the potatoes to the meat and cook gently for 5 minutes. Taste and adjust the seasoning, adding salt if necessary. Garnish with the almonds.

Picadillo can be served with rice or as a filling for Tacos (see page 40), Empanadas (see page 26) and similar dishes.

Cooking time: about 50 minutes
Serves 4 to 6

Pork with Lentils and Pineapple

METRIC/IMPERIAL
1 kg/2 lb lean pork,
  cut into 4 cm/
  1½ inch cubes
1 × 298 g/10½ oz can
  condensed onion
  soup
1 soup can water
2 medium cloves
  garlic, crushed
450 ml/¾ pint
  vegetable juice
350 g/12 oz dried
  orange lentils
2 tablespoons oil
1 large under-ripe
  banana, sliced
1 × 225 g/8 oz can
  pineapple chunks,
  drained
soured cream to
  serve

AMERICAN
2 lb lean pork, cut into
  1½ inch cubes
1 can (10½ oz)
  condensed onion
  soup
1 soup can water
2 medium-size cloves
  garlic, minced
2 cups vegetable juice
1½ cups dried lentils
2 tablespoons oil
1 large plantain or
  green-tipped
  banana, sliced
1 cup canned and
  drained pineapple
  chunks
sour cream to serve

Place the pork, onion soup, water and garlic in a large heavy pan. Bring to the boil, cover and simmer for 1 hour. Add the vegetable juice and lentils. Simmer for a further hour or until the pork and lentils are cooked, stirring occasionally.

Meanwhile heat the oil in a frying pan, add the banana and pineapple and fry until brown. Add to the pork mixture. Heat through, stirring occasionally. Serve with soured cream.
Cooking time: about 2¼ hours
Serves 6

Barbecued Mexican Burgers

METRIC/IMPERIAL
25 g/1 oz butter
1 large onion,
  chopped
450 g/1 lb minced
  beef
2 × 283 g/10 oz cans
  red kidney beans
120 ml/4 fl oz bottled
  barbecue sauce
½ teaspoon salt
8 hamburger buns,
  split and toasted

AMERICAN
2 tablespoons butter
1 large onion,
  chopped
1 lb ground beef
1 can (1 lb 12 oz) red
  kidney beans
½ cup bottled
  barbecue sauce
½ teaspoon salt
8 hamburger buns,
  split and toasted

Melt the butter in a frying pan, add the onion and fry for 5 minutes until soft. Add the beef and cook until browned, breaking up the meat as it cooks. Pour off any excess fat. Stir in the beans, barbecue sauce and salt. Simmer for 5 minutes. Serve on the toasted buns.
Cooking time: 20 minutes
Serves 8

Southwestern Stew with Corn

METRIC/IMPERIAL
2 tablespoons oil
450 g/1 lb stewing or
  braising steak, cut
  into 1 cm/½ inch
  cubes
100 g/4 oz onion,
  chopped
1 × 793 g/1 lb 12 oz
  can tomatoes
250 ml/8 fl oz water
1 tablespoon chilli
  powder
2 teaspoons crushed
  oregano leaves
2 teaspoons salt
½ teaspoon sugar
½ teaspoon garlic
  powder
1 × 425 g/15 oz can
  red kidney beans,
  drained
8 pieces frozen corn
  on the cob

AMERICAN
2 tablespoons oil
1 lb beef for stew, cut
  into ½ inch cubes
1 cup chopped onion
1 can (1 lb 12 oz)
  tomatoes
1 cup water
1 tablespoon chili
  powder
2 teaspoons crushed
  oregano leaves
2 teaspoons salt
½ teaspoon sugar
½ teaspoon garlic
  powder
1 can (15¼ oz) red
  kidney beans,
  drained
1 package (8 pieces)
  frozen corn on the
  cob

Heat the oil in a large pan, add the beef and onion and fry until the meat is well browned. Add the tomatoes with their juice, water, chilli powder, oregano, salt, sugar and garlic powder. Cover and simmer for about 2 hours, stirring occasionally, until the meat is tender. Add the beans and frozen corn and bring to the boil. Cover and simmer for a further 20 minutes.
Cooking time: about 2½ hours
Serves 4

Beef and Pork Chilli

METRIC/IMPERIAL	AMERICAN
2 rashers lean bacon, diced	2 slices Canadian bacon, diced
450 g/1 lb braising steak, cut into 1 cm/½ inch cubes	1 lb lean beef for stew, cut into ½ inch cubes
450 g/1 lb lean hand of pork, cut into 1 cm/½ inch cubes	1 lb lean pork shoulder, cut into ½ inch cubes
2 medium onions, sliced	2 medium-size onions, sliced
2 cloves garlic, crushed	2 cloves garlic, minced
½ teaspoon dried oregano	½ teaspoon dried oregano
1 teaspoon salt	1 teaspoon salt
½ teaspoon ground cumin	½ teaspoon ground cumin
½ teaspoon ground coriander	½ teaspoon ground coriander
2 green chillies, seeded and chopped	2 green chilies, seeded and chopped
175 ml/6 fl oz beef stock	¾ cup beef stock
175 ml/6 fl oz dry red wine	¾ cup dry red wine
1 × 227 g/8 oz can tomatoes	1 can (10 oz) tomatoes
1 green pepper, cored, seeded and sliced	1 green pepper, seeded and sliced
1 × 225 g/8 oz can tomato sauce	1 can (8 oz) tomato sauce

Place the bacon in a pan and fry until fairly crisp. Add the meats, onions and garlic and fry until the meat is brown. Stir in the oregano, salt, cumin, coriander, chillies, stock, wine, tomatoes, green pepper and tomato sauce. Cover and simmer for 1½ hours or until the meat is tender.
Cooking time: about 1¾ hours
Serves 8

Pork Chops Veracruz

METRIC/IMPERIAL	AMERICAN
2 tablespoons oil	2 tablespoons oil
6 pork chops, 2-2.5 cm/ ¾-1 inch thick	6 pork chops, ¾-1 inch thick
1 tablespoon plain flour	1 tablespoon all-purpose flour
1 tablespoon brown sugar	1 tablespoon brown sugar
1 teaspoon dry mustard	1 teaspoon dry mustard
1 teaspoon salt	1 teaspoon salt
1 clove garlic, crushed	1 clove garlic, minced
2 medium onions, sliced	2 medium-size onions, sliced
120 ml/4 fl oz dry white wine	½ cup dry white wine
about 120 ml/4 fl oz water	about ½ cup water
1 medium green pepper, cored, seeded and chopped	1 medium-size green pepper, seeded and chopped
1 medium red pepper, cored, seeded and chopped	1 medium-size red pepper, seeded and chopped
2-3 tablespoons coarsely chopped pimento	2-3 tablespoons coarsely chopped pimiento

Heat the oil in a large frying pan, add the pork chops and fry, turning to brown well on both sides. Drain off excess fat. Sprinkle with the flour, brown sugar, mustard, salt and garlic. Add the onions and wine; cover and cook over a low heat for about 1 hour until the chops are tender. Add extra water if needed and spoon the sauce over the chops several times during cooking. Add the green and red peppers to the pork 15 minutes before the end of cooking time. Top with pimento and serve with boiled rice.
Cooking time: about 1 hour
Serves 6

Pork Chops Veracruz
(Photograph: Uncle Ben's Rice Inc.)

Pork Chops in Hot Tomato Sauce

METRIC/IMPERIAL
2-4 small dried red chillies
1 × 298 g/10½ oz can condensed tomato soup
50 g/2 oz onion, chopped
4 tablespoons wine vinegar
2 medium cloves garlic, crushed
½ teaspoon crushed oregano leaves
¼ teaspoon ground cumin
1 kg/2 lb thinly sliced pork chops (8-10)
lime slices to garnish (optional)

AMERICAN
2-4 small dried red chilies
1 can (11 oz) condensed tomato soup
½ cup chopped onion
¼ cup wine vinegar
2 medium-size cloves garlic, minced
½ teaspoon crushed oregano leaves
¼ teaspoon ground cumin
2 lb thinly sliced pork chops (8-10)
lime slices for garnish (optional)

Remove the stems and seeds from the chillies. Place the chillies in a pan and add enough water to cover. Cover and simmer for 5 minutes; drain.

For the marinade, place the chillies, soup, onion, vinegar, garlic, oregano and cumin in a blender and blend until smooth.

Arrange the pork chops in a shallow dish. Pour the marinade over and chill for 4 hours or more, turning the chops occasionally.

Place the pork chops in a frying pan and add the marinade. Cover and cook, stirring occasionally, over a low heat for about 20 minutes until the chops are cooked.

Serve the chops on a bed of rice with the remaining marinade. Garnish with lime slices, if liked.
Cooking time: about 25 minutes
Serves 4 to 5

South-of-the-Border Chilli

METRIC/IMPERIAL
1 × 650 g/1 lb 4 oz can pineapple chunks
1 tablespoon oil
750 g/1½ lb hand of pork, cut into 2.5 cm/1 inch cubes
1 teaspoon garlic salt
1 teaspoon salt
¼ teaspoon ground black pepper
1 large onion, chopped
1 tablespoon chilli powder
1 × 225 g/8 oz can tomato sauce
1 × 175 g/6 oz can tomato purée
120 ml/4 fl oz beef stock
1 green pepper, cored, seeded and sliced

AMERICAN
1 can (1 lb 4 oz) pineapple chunks
1 tablespoon oil
1½ lb pork shoulder, cut into 1 inch cubes
1 teaspoon garlic salt
1 teaspoon salt
¼ teaspoon ground black pepper
1 large onion, chopped
1 tablespoon chili powder
1 can (8 oz) tomato sauce
1 can (6 oz) tomato paste
½ cup beef stock
1 green pepper, seeded and sliced

Drain the pineapple, reserving the juice. Heat the oil in a large frying pan, add the pork and brown well. Season with garlic salt, salt and pepper.

Add the onion and fry for 1 minute. Sprinkle over the chilli powder. Add the tomato sauce, tomato purée (paste), reserved pineapple juice and beef stock; mix well. Partly cover and simmer for 1 hour. Add the pineapple and green pepper. Simmer for a further 10 minutes. Serve hot with rice.
Cooking time: about 1¼ hours
Serves 6

Chicken Yucatan

METRIC/IMPERIAL	AMERICAN
1 × 298 g/10½ oz can condensed cream of chicken soup	1 can (10¾ oz) condensed cream of chicken soup
1 onion, chopped	1 onion, chopped
40 g/1½ oz blanched almonds, chopped	⅓ cup chopped almonds
4 medium cloves garlic, crushed	4 medium-size cloves garlic, minced
1 tablespoon vinegar	1 tablespoon vinegar
½ teaspoon crushed oregano leaves	½ teaspoon crushed oregano leaves
¼ teaspoon ground black pepper	¼ teaspoon ground black pepper
25 g/1 oz lard	2 tablespoons lard
4 chicken portions	4 chicken portions
2-4 canned chillies or pimentos	2-4 canned jalapeno chilies

Blend soup, onion, almonds, garlic, vinegar, oregano and pepper in a blender until smooth.

Heat the lard in a frying pan, add the chicken and fry until brown on all sides. Pour off any excess fat. Add the soup mixture and chillies to the chicken. Cover and simmer for 45 minutes until chicken is tender, stirring occasionally.
Cooking time: about 1 hour
Serves 4

Orange Chicken

METRIC/IMPERIAL	AMERICAN
1 teaspoon salt	1 teaspoon salt
¼ teaspoon ground cinnamon	¼ teaspoon ground cinnamon
⅛ teaspoon ground cloves	⅛ teaspoon ground cloves
6 chicken portions	6 chicken portions
2 tablespoons oil	2 tablespoons oil
1 onion, chopped	1 cup chopped onion
1 clove garlic, crushed	1 clove garlic, minced
150 ml/¼ pint orange juice	½ cup orange juice
150 ml/¼ pint chicken stock	½ cup chicken stock or broth
2 tablespoons raisins	2 tablespoons seedless raisins
2 green chillies, seeded and sliced	1 can (4 oz) whole green chilies, sliced
50 g/2 oz slivered almonds	⅓ cup slivered almonds
2 oranges, peeled and thinly sliced	2 oranges, peeled and thinly sliced

Mix the salt, cinnamon and cloves together and rub all over the chicken. Heat the oil in a large frying pan or flameproof casserole, add the chicken and fry until brown on all sides. Remove the chicken and pour off any excess fat. Add the onion and garlic to the pan and fry until the onion is soft.

Return the chicken to the pan. Stir in the orange juice, chicken stock, raisins and chillies. Cover and simmer for 1 hour or until the chicken is tender. Add the almonds and oranges and heat through for about 5 minutes.
Cooking time: 1¼ hours
Serves 6

Acapulco Pot Roast

METRIC/IMPERIAL	AMERICAN
50 g/2 oz plain flour	½ cup all-purpose flour
1 teaspoon chilli powder	1 teaspoon chili powder
1 tablespoon paprika	1 tablespoon paprika
2 teaspoons salt	2 teaspoons salt
1.75-2.25 kg/4-5 lb rolled brisket of beef or chuck steak	4-5 lb beef blade pot roast
40 g/1½ oz lard	3 tablespoons shortening
2 medium onions	2 medium-size onions
16 cloves	16 cloves
5 tablespoons water	⅓ cup water
1 cinnamon stick	1 cinnamon stick

Combine 25 g/1 oz (¼ cup) of the flour, with the chilli powder, paprika and salt. Dredge the meat with the seasoned flour.

Melt the lard (shortening) in a heavy pan or flameproof casserole, add the beef and fry until brown on all sides. Pour off any excess fat. Stud each onion with 8 cloves. Add the water, onions and cinnamon stick to the meat. Cover and simmer for 2½ to 3 hours or until the meat is tender.

Remove the meat to a warm serving plate. Discard the onions and cinnamon stick. Measure the cooking liquid and add water to make 450 ml/¾ pint (2 cups). Mix the remaining flour with 4 tablespoons water until smooth. Add to the cooking liquid and cook, stirring continuously, until thickened. Serve this gravy with the meat.
Cooking time: 2¾ to 3¼ hours
Serves 6 to 8

Turkey Mole

METRIC/IMPERIAL

1 turkey, weighing
    2.75-3.5 kg/6-8 lb,
    cut into serving
    pieces
1 onion, stuck with
    3 cloves
2 sticks celery
2 parsley sprigs
salt and freshly
    ground pepper
75 g/3 oz lard or
    6 tablespoons olive
    oil

Sauce:
5 chillies mulatos (see
    note)
4 small hot dried
    chillies
4 chillies pastillas
1 onion, chopped
4 large tomatoes,
    skinned and
    chopped
40 g/1½ oz sesame
    seeds
40 g/1½ oz pumpkin
    seeds
¼ teaspoon anise
    seeds
50 g/2 oz shelled
    unsalted peanuts
40 g/1½ oz raisins or
    currants
3 cloves garlic,
    crushed
1 slice French bread,
    toasted
1 corn tortilla, cut into
    strips (see page 40)
2.5 cm/1 inch piece
    cinnamon stick
7 peppercorns
3 cloves
50 g/2 oz Mexican
    chocolate or other
    sweetened
    chocolate, grated

AMERICAN

1 turkey, weighing
    6-8 lb, cut into
    serving pieces
1 onion, stuck with
    3 cloves
2 stalks celery
2 parsley sprigs
salt and freshly
    ground pepper
6 tablespoons
    shortening or
    olive oil

Sauce:
5 chilies mulatos (see
    note)
4 chilies anchos
4 chilies pastillas
1 onion, chopped
4 large tomatoes,
    peeled and
    chopped
¼ cup sesame seeds
½ cup pumpkin seeds
¼ teaspoon anise
    seeds
½ cup shelled
    unsalted peanuts
¼ cup raisins or
    currants
3 cloves garlic,
    minced
1 slice French bread,
    toasted
1 corn tortilla, cut into
    strips (see page 40)
1 inch piece
    cinnamon stick
7 peppercorns
3 cloves
2 squares (1 oz each)
    Mexican chocolate
    or other good
    quality sweetened
    chocolate, grated

For the sauce, soak the chillies in sufficient water to cover overnight. Drain, remove the stems, then grind the chilli seeds and pulp to a paste; set aside.

Put the turkey pieces in a flameproof casserole and add just enough water to cover. Add the onion, celery, parsley and salt and pepper to taste. Bring to the boil, skim and lower the heat. Cover and simmer gently for 1½ to 2 hours until the turkey is tender. Drain the turkey and reserve 450 ml/¾ pint (2 cups) of the stock. Pat the turkey dry with kitchen paper towels.

Heat half of the lard (shortening) or oil in a heavy frying pan, add the turkey pieces and fry, turning until evenly browned. Transfer to a large flameproof casserole.

Grind together all of the sauce ingredients except the chocolate and chilli paste, using a pestle and mortar. Alternatively, purée the mixture, adding a little of the reserved stock, in a blender until smooth. Stir in the chilli paste.

Heat the remaining lard (shortening) or oil in a pan, add the sauce mixture and reduce the heat. Add the chocolate and stir constantly for 5 minutes or until thoroughly blended. Stir in the reserved turkey stock. Cover and cook gently for 35 to 40 minutes, stirring occasionally, until the liquor thickens.

Pour the sauce over the turkey and leave over a low heat for 20 minutes or until the turkey is hot. Serve this special occasion dish with Christmas Salad (see page 53).

Cooking time: 2¾ to 3¼ hours

Serves 8 to 10

Note: if you are unable to obtain the special chilli peppers for the sauce, substitute a mixture of chillies and red or green peppers to taste.

Turkey Mole; Christmas Salad (page 53)

Chilli Chicken Casserole

METRIC/IMPERIAL	AMERICAN
2 tablespoons oil	2 tablespoons oil
1 onion, chopped	1 onion, chopped
1 clove garlic, crushed	1 clove garlic, minced
1 × 397 g/14 oz can tomatoes	1 can (16 oz) tomatoes
1 × 225 g/8 oz can tomato sauce	1 can (8 oz) tomato sauce
1 pepper, cored, seeded and chopped	1 pepper, seeded and chopped
2-4 teaspoons chilli powder	2-4 teaspoons chili powder
1 teaspoon chopped oregano leaves	1 teaspoon chopped oregano leaves
⅛ teaspoon salt	⅛ teaspoon salt
1 × 340 g/12 oz can sweetcorn kernels	1 can (16 oz) whole kernel corn
1 tablespoon cornflour	1 tablespoon cornstarch
75 g/3 oz stoned black olives, sliced	½ cup pitted ripe olives, sliced
750 g/1½ lb boned cooked chicken, cut into chunks	1½ lb boned cooked chicken, cut into chunks
6 rashers streaky bacon	6 bacon slices

Heat the oil in a pan, add the onion and garlic and fry for 5 minutes. Stir in the tomatoes with their juice, tomato sauce, pepper, chilli powder, oregano and salt.

Drain the corn, reserving the liquid. Mix the cornflour (cornstarch) with the reserved corn liquid and add to the pan. Simmer, uncovered, for 15 minutes, stirring occasionally.

Remove the pan from the heat and add the olives. Taste for seasoning, adding additional salt and chilli powder, if liked. Place a layer of corn and chicken in a greased casserole. Spoon over enough sauce to cover. Repeat the layers, ending with corn. Arrange the bacon over the top.

Cook in a preheated moderately hot oven (200°C/400°F, Gas Mark 6) for 20 minutes or until the bacon is crisp and the casserole is bubbling.

Cooking time: 40 minutes
Serves 8

Chicken and Courgettes (Zucchini)

METRIC/IMPERIAL	AMERICAN
2 tablespoons oil	2 tablespoons oil
2 cloves garlic, crushed	2 cloves garlic, minced
1 × 1.5 kg/3 lb chicken, cut into 6 pieces	1 × 3 lb frying chicken, cut into 6 pieces
2 tablespoons plain flour	2 tablespoons all-purpose flour
2 teaspoons salt	2 teaspoons salt
½ teaspoon ground cumin	½ teaspoon ground cumin
¼ teaspoon ground black pepper	¼ teaspoon ground black pepper
1 × 397 g/14 oz can tomatoes	1 can (16 oz) tomatoes
1 medium onion, chopped	1 medium-size onion, chopped
225 g/8 oz long-grain rice	1 cup long-grain rice
450 g/1 lb courgettes, cut into 5 mm/ ¼ inch slices	1 lb zucchini, cut into ¼ inch slices
1 × 198 g/7 oz can sweetcorn kernels, drained	1 can (7 oz) whole kernel corn, drained

Heat the oil and garlic in a large frying pan, add the chicken and fry, turning to brown well on all sides. Sprinkle the chicken with the flour, 1 teaspoon of the salt, the cumin and pepper. Drain the tomatoes, reserving the juice. Add onion and tomato juice to the chicken; cover and cook over a low heat for about 30 minutes.

Meanwhile cook the rice in boiling salted water. Add the courgettes (zucchini), tomatoes and remaining salt to the chicken; cover and cook for about 15 minutes until the chicken and courgettes (zucchini) are tender. Skim off any excess fat. Stir the corn into the hot cooked rice. Serve the chicken with the rice.

Cooking time: 1 hour
Serves 6

Chicken in Spicy Sauce

METRIC/IMPERIAL
1 × 298 g/10½ oz can
  condensed chicken
  soup, or fresh
  chicken stock
1 × 100 g/4 oz can
  tomatoes with
  green chillies or
  canned tomatoes
  with 1 chopped
  fresh green chilli
1 corn tortilla, torn
  into pieces (see
  page 40)
2 tablespoons smooth
  peanut butter
1 teaspoon chilli
  powder
1 medium clove
  garlic, crushed
½ teaspoon ground
  cinnamon
¼ teaspoon ground
  cloves
¼ teaspoon ground
  black pepper
25 g/1 oz lard
4 chicken portions
coriander leaves to
  garnish (optional)

AMERICAN
1 can (10¾ oz)
  condensed chicken
  broth
1 can (4 oz) tomatoes
  with green chilies
1 corn tortilla, torn
  into pieces (see
  page 40)
2 tablespoons creamy
  peanut butter
1 teaspoon chili
  powder
1 medium-size clove
  garlic, minced
½ teaspoon ground
  cinnamon
¼ teaspoon ground
  cloves
¼ teaspoon ground
  black pepper
2 tablespoons
  shortening
4 chicken portions
coriander leaves for
  garnish (optional)

Place the soup, stock or broth, tomatoes with green chillies, tortilla pieces, peanut butter, chilli powder, garlic, cinnamon, cloves and black pepper in a blender. Blend until smooth.

Melt the fat in a frying pan, add the chicken and fry until brown on all sides. Pour off any excess fat. Add the soup mixture. Cover and cook over a low heat for 45 minutes or until the chicken is tender, stirring occasionally. Garnish with coriander leaves, if liked.
Cooking time: about 1 hour
Serves 4

Mexican Chicken Omelette

METRIC/IMPERIAL
50 g/2 oz butter
50 g/2 oz onion, finely
  chopped
½ clove garlic,
  crushed
350 g/12 oz tomatoes,
  diced
225 g/8 oz cooked
  chicken, diced
2 teaspoons chilli
  powder
1¼ teaspoons salt
6 eggs
2 tablespoons milk
⅛ teaspoon ground
  black pepper

AMERICAN
¼ cup butter
½ cup finely chopped
  onion
½ clove garlic,
  minced
1½ cups diced
  tomatoes
1 cup diced cooked
  chicken
2 teaspoons chili
  powder
1¼ teaspoons salt
6 eggs
2 tablespoons milk
⅛ teaspoon ground
  black pepper

Melt 40 g/1½ oz (3 tablespoons) of the butter in a pan, add the onion and garlic and fry for 5 minutes. Add the tomatoes, chicken, chilli powder and ¾ teaspoon of the salt. Cook, stirring continuously, over a low heat until hot. Cover and keep warm.

Lightly beat the eggs in a bowl. Stir in the milk, black pepper and remaining salt. Melt the remaining butter in a frying pan or omelette pan, add the egg mixture and cook over a moderate heat. As the mixture sets at the edge, tilt the pan and, with a wooden spoon, push back the cooked egg gently allowing the uncooked egg to flow to the bottom. Spoon the hot chicken mixture down one side of the omelette. Carefully loosen the omelette from the bottom of the pan and fold in half. Turn out on to a serving plate and serve immediately.
Cooking time: about 20 minutes
Serves 4

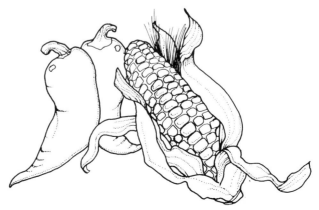

Tortillas, Tacos & Enchiladas

Enchiladas de Pollo

METRIC/IMPERIAL
2 eggs, beaten
2 tablespoons water
¼ teaspoon ground
   cinnamon
12 corn tortillas,
   about 10-13 cm/4-5
   inches in diameter
   (see page 40)
oil for frying
Sauce:
4 tablespoons olive
   oil
6 tomatoes, skinned
   and chopped
1 onion, chopped
½ teaspoon ground
   cumin
1 green or red
   pepper, cored,
   seeded and
   chopped
salt and freshly
   ground pepper
Filling:
225 g/8 oz cooked
   chicken, turkey,
   pork or veal,
   chopped
40 g/1½ oz raisins,
   chopped
50 g/2 oz blanched
   almonds, chopped
2 tablespoons
   chopped green
   olives

AMERICAN
2 eggs, beaten
2 tablespoons water
¼ teaspoon ground
   cinnamon
12 corn tortillas,
   about 4-5 inches in
   diameter (see page
   40)
oil for frying
Sauce:
¼ cup olive oil
6 tomatoes, peeled
   and chopped
1 onion, chopped
½ teaspoon ground
   cumin
1 green or red
   pepper, seeded and
   chopped
salt and freshly
   ground pepper
Filling:
1 cup chopped
   cooked chicken,
   turkey, pork or veal
¼ cup raisins,
   chopped
½ cup chopped
   almonds
2 tablespoons
   chopped green
   olives

Garnish:
1 Spanish onion,
   thinly sliced into
   rings
1 small lettuce, finely
   shredded (optional)
few radishes, thinly
   sliced (optional)

Garnish:
1 Spanish onion,
   thinly sliced into
   rings
1 small head lettuce,
   finely shredded
   (optional)
few radishes, thinly
   sliced (optional)

To make the sauce: heat the oil in a frying pan. Stir in the tomatoes, onion, cumin and chopped pepper and fry until the vegetables are tender. Add salt and pepper to taste. Remove from the heat and keep warm.

Combine all the filling ingredients in a bowl and mix thoroughly.

Beat the eggs with the water and cinnamon until frothy, then dip each tortilla into this mixture to coat. Place some of the filling in the centre of each tortilla, roll up and secure with wooden cocktail sticks (toothpicks).

Heat the oil in the frying pan, add the enchiladas and quickly fry for about 2 minutes on each side until golden brown. Drain on kitchen paper towels.

Arrange the enchiladas on a heated serving dish and pour over the sauce. Serve hot, garnished with onion rings and lettuce and radishes, if liked.

Cooking time: about 15 minutes
Serves 4 to 6

Enchiladas de Pollo

Corn Tortillas

METRIC/IMPERIAL	AMERICAN
275 g/10 oz cornmeal flour (masa harina)	2 cups cornmeal flour (masa harina)
pinch of salt	pinch of salt
about 350 ml/12 fl oz warm water	about 1½ cups warm water

Place the cornmeal flour (masa harina) and salt in a bowl. Add the water gradually, kneading until a smooth soft dough is formed. Divide into 14 pieces and leave to stand for 1 hour.

Place each piece of dough between 2 sheets of cling film (plastic wrap). Flatten with a rolling pin to thin cakes, 13 cm/5 inches in diameter.

Heat an ungreased heavy frying pan. When hot, place a tortilla in the pan. Cook for about 1 minute or until golden speckles appear on the surface. Turn the tortilla and cook the other side for 1 to 1½ minutes. Wrap in a warm cloth and keep hot while cooking the remainder.
Makes 14
Note: if the tortillas become cool and dry, moisten with a little water and reheat in the frying pan before use.

Flour Tortillas

METRIC/IMPERIAL	AMERICAN
225 g/8 oz plain flour	2 cups all-purpose flour
1 teaspoon salt	1 teaspoon salt
¾ teaspoon baking powder	¾ teaspoon baking powder
50 g/2 oz lard	¼ cup shortening
about 150 ml/¼ pint water	½ cup plus 2 tablespoons water

Place the flour, salt and baking powder in a bowl. Add the lard (shortening) and rub in with the fingertips until the mixture resembles fine breadcrumbs. Stir in the water and knead briefly until the dough forms a smooth ball. Cover and leave to rest for 15 minutes.

Pull off a 4 cm (1½ inch) ball of dough and roll out on a floured board to 20 cm (8 inches) in diameter. Cook in an ungreased frying pan on each side for about 1½ minutes. As bubbles form, press down with a spatula until the tortilla has brown spots. Tortillas should be cooked but still soft. Wrap in a warm cloth or foil and keep hot while cooking the remainder.
Makes about 10

Red Chilli Sauce

METRIC/IMPERIAL	AMERICAN
5 small dried red chillies, crumbled	5 small dried red chillies, crumbled
3 tablespoons boiling water	3 tablespoons boiling water
1 × 397 g/14 oz can tomatoes, chopped and drained, reserving the juice	1 can (16 oz) tomatoes, chopped and drained, reserving the juice
4 tablespoons oil	4 tablespoons oil
2 onions, chopped	2 onions, chopped
2 cloves garlic, crushed	2 cloves garlic, minced
3 tablespoons tomato purée	3 tablespoons tomato paste
1 teaspoon ground cumin	1 teaspoon ground cumin
1 teaspoon ground coriander	1 teaspoon ground coriander
1½ tablespoons wine vinegar	1½ tablespoons wine vinegar
1 teaspoon sugar	1 teaspoon sugar

Place the chillies, water and tomatoes in a blender and blend until smooth. Pour into a jug.

Heat the oil in a pan, add the onions and garlic and fry until soft. Stir in the chilli and tomato mixture, reserved tomato juice, tomato purée (paste), cumin, coriander, vinegar and sugar. Cover and simmer for 10 minutes.

Use as part of a dish or serve with meat, or as an accompaniment to tortillas, tacos, etc.
Cooking time: 15 to 20 minutes
Makes about 600 ml/1 pint (2½ cups)

Tacos

METRIC/IMPERIAL	AMERICAN
oil for frying	oil for frying
corn tortillas (see left)	corn tortillas (see left)

Heat the oil, about 1.5 cm/¾ inch deep, in a frying pan. When hot, add a tortilla and, with tongs, fold over one side, keeping a good space between the upper and lower sides for the filling. Fry the tortilla, turning occasionally, until crisp. Remove from the oil and keep hot while making the other taco shells.

Tacos are a snack or appetizer. For a light main course, serve 2 tacos with substantial fillings per person.

Green Tomato Sauce

METRIC/IMPERIAL
2 tablespoons oil
1 large onion,
   chopped
450 g/1 lb canned
   Mexican green
   tomatoes
   (tomatillos)
2 fresh or canned
   green chillies,
   chopped
1 tablespoon finely
   chopped coriander
   leaves
250 ml/8 fl oz chicken
   stock

AMERICAN
2 tablespoons oil
1 large onion,
   chopped
1 lb canned Mexican
   green tomatoes
   (tomatillos)
2 fresh or canned
   green chilies,
   chopped
1 tablespoon finely
   chopped coriander
   leaves
1 cup chicken stock or
   broth

Heat the oil in a frying pan, add the onion and fry until soft. Put the onion, tomatoes, chillies and coriander leaves into a blender and blend until smooth. Transfer to a pan and stir over a low heat. Gradually add the chicken stock, stirring. Simmer for 5 minutes.

Serve as an accompaniment to tacos and enchiladas, or with roast or grilled (broiled) meats.
Cooking time: 15 minutes
Makes about 750 ml/1¼ pints (3 cups)

Fiesta Burritos

METRIC/IMPERIAL
10-12 flour tortillas
   (see page 40)
1 × 30 g/1¼ oz
   envelope taco or
   Chilli con Carne
   seasoning mix
350 ml/12 fl oz tomato
   juice
1 tablespoon oil
225 g/8 oz minced
   beef
Refried Beans (see
   page 47)
75-100 g/3-4 oz
   lettuce, chopped
225 g/8 oz Cheddar
   cheese, grated

AMERICAN
10-12 flour tortillas
   (see page 40)
1 envelope (1¼ oz)
   taco seasoning mix
1½ cups tomato juice
1 tablespoon oil
8 oz ground beef
1 can (15 oz) Refried
   Beans or about
   225 g/8 oz
   home-made (see
   page 47)
1½ cups finely
   chopped lettuce
2 cups grated
   Cheddar cheese

Wrap the tortillas in foil and place in a preheated moderate oven (180°C/350°F, Gas Mark 4) while preparing the filling.

Stir the seasoning mix, tomato juice and oil together. Place the beef in a frying pan and fry until brown and cooked, breaking up the meat as it cooks. Pour off any excess fat. Stir in the beans and 120 ml/4 fl oz (½ cup) of the tomato mixture. Cover and simmer for 5 to 10 minutes, stirring occasionally, until hot.

Place a generous spoonful of the beef and bean filling on each tortilla; sprinkle with lettuce and about 175 g/6 oz (1½ cups) of the cheese and roll up each tortilla. Place, seam-side down, in a greased shallow casserole. Pour the remaining tomato mixture over and top with remaining cheese. Cover and bake in a preheated moderate oven (180°C/350°F, Gas Mark 4) for 20 minutes until hot.
Cooking time: 40 minutes
Serves 6

Taco Dogs

METRIC/IMPERIAL
450 g/1 lb minced beef
50 g/2 oz onion,
   chopped
120 ml/4 fl oz tomato
   ketchup
120 ml/4 fl oz water
1 × 30 g/1¼ oz
   envelope taco or
   Chilli con Carne
   seasoning mix
8-10 tacos (page 40)
450 g/1 lb frankfurters
   (8-10)
8-10 tablespoons
   grated cheese

AMERICAN
1 lb ground beef
½ cup chopped onion
½ cup tomato
   ketchup
½ cup water
1 envelope (1¼ oz)
   taco seasoning mix
8-10 tacos (see page
   40)
1 lb frankfurters (8-10)
8-10 tablespoons
   grated Cheddar
   cheese

Place the beef in a frying pan and fry until brown and cooked, breaking up the meat as it cooks. Pour off any excess fat. Add the onion, ketchup, water and seasoning mix and cook over a low heat for 5 to 7 minutes.

Divide the beef mixture into 8 to 10 equal portions (the same number as frankfurters). Place half of each portion of beef mixture in a taco. Place a frankfurter over the meat in each and add the remaining beef mixture. Top each filled taco shell with 1 tablespoon grated cheese. Cook in a preheated moderate oven (180°C/350°F, Gas Mark 4) for 10 minutes.
Cooking time: about 25 minutes
Makes 8 to 10

Quesadilla

METRIC/IMPERIAL	AMERICAN
4 flour tortillas (see page 40)	4 flour tortillas (see page 40)
225 g/8 oz Cheddar cheese, grated	2 cups grated Cheddar or Monterey Jack cheese
225 g/8 oz cooked chicken, chopped	1 cup chopped cooked chicken
4 green chillies, chopped	4 green chilies, chopped
1 small onion, chopped	1 small onion, chopped
oil for frying	oil for frying
To serve:	**To serve:**
soured cream	sour cream

Wrap the tortillas in foil and warm in the oven to soften. Remove and unwrap. Lay the tortillas flat. Divide the cheese and chicken and spread on to half of each tortilla. Sprinkle with the chillies and onion. Fold the tortillas over in half and seal the edges or secure with wooden cocktail sticks (toothpicks). Heat about 2.5 cm/1 inch oil in a frying pan, add the folded tortillas and fry for about 2 minutes on each side until lightly browned. Drain on kitchen paper towels. Serve with soured cream.
Cooking time: about 10 minutes
Makes 4

Chimichangas

METRIC/IMPERIAL	AMERICAN
flour tortillas (see page 40)	flour tortillas (see page 40)
Picadillo (see page 28)	Picadillo (see page 28)
lard or oil for frying	lard or oil for frying

Wrap the tortillas in foil and warm in the oven for a few minutes to soften. Place about 100 g/4 oz (½ cup) of the meat mixture in the centre of each tortilla. Fold in the sides, then roll. Heat about 2.5-4 cm/1-1½ inches lard or oil in a frying pan. Place the filled tortillas seam-side down in the pan and fry for 2 to 3 minutes, pressing down with a spatula to keep from unrolling, until crisp and lightly browned. Turn to brown both sides. Drain on paper towels.
Cooking time: about 5 minutes
Makes about 10

Tacos with Chillies and Cream

METRIC/IMPERIAL	AMERICAN
1 dried chilli	1 chili chipotle (or other dried chili)
1 clove garlic	1 clove garlic
4 tablespoons oil	¼ cup olive oil
2 large onions, coarsely chopped	2 large onions, coarsely chopped
4 tomatoes, skinned and chopped	4 tomatoes, peeled and chopped
1 bay leaf, crumbled	1 bay leaf, crumbled
2 tablespoons chopped coriander leaves or parsley	2 tablespoons chopped coriander leaves or parsley
250 ml/8 fl oz rich beef stock	1 cup rich beef stock
salt	salt
2 fresh chillies, skinned, seeded and cut into strips	2 poblano chilies, peeled, seeded and cut into strips
120 ml/4 fl oz soured cream	½ cup sour cream
12 corn tortillas, 10-13 cm/4-5 inches in diameter (page 40)	12 corn tortillas, 4-5 inches in diameter (see page 40)
oil or lard for frying	oil or lard for frying
25-50 g/1-2 oz mild cheese, grated	⅓ cup grated mild Cheddar cheese

To make the sauce: soak dried chilli overnight in just enough water to cover. Add garlic and crush the mixture to a paste, using a pestle and mortar. Heat 2 tablespoons of the oil in a pan, add half of the onions and fry until golden. Add two of the tomatoes, the herbs, chilli mixture and stock. Cook over a low heat, stirring until thickened. Add salt to taste.

For the filling: heat the remaining 2 tablespoons oil in a pan, add the rest of the onion and fry for a few minutes. Add the fresh chillies and cook until just tender, but not mushy. Add the remaining tomatoes and cook gently for 2 minutes. Stir in cream and heat through; do not allow to boil. Season with salt.

Divide the filling between the tortillas; placing it in the centre of each one. Fold over the edges and secure with wooden cocktail sticks (toothpicks). Heat a heavy frying pan with just enough oil or lard to cover the bottom. Place tortillas in the pan, sealed side down, and fry until golden. Turn and fry other side.

Transfer to a heated serving dish. Spoon over sauce, sprinkle with cheese and serve hot.
Cooking time: about 25 minutes
Serves 4 to 6

Tacos with Chillies and Cream

Flautas

METRIC/IMPERIAL	AMERICAN
8 corn tortillas (see page 40)	8 corn tortillas (see page 40)
Bean and cheese filling:	**Bean and cheese filling:**
400 g/14 oz Refried Beans (see page 47)	14 oz Refried Beans (see page 47)
2-4 green chillies, chopped	1 can (7 oz) diced green chilies
50 g/2 oz wheat germ	½ cup wheat germ
50 g/2 oz onion, chopped	¼ cup minced onion
25 g/1 oz almonds, toasted and chopped	¼ cup chopped almonds, toasted
100 g/4 oz Cheddar cheese, grated	1 cup grated Monterey Jack cheese
oil for frying	oil for frying

Wrap the tortillas in foil and warm in the oven to soften.

Meanwhile, place the beans and chillies in a pan and heat through, stirring occasionally. Mix in the wheat germ, onion, almonds and cheese.

Overlap 2 tortillas for each flauta. Spoon the bean and cheese filling down the centre. Roll tightly to form a long tube. Secure with wooden cocktail sticks (toothpicks). Heat the oil, about 2.5 cm/1 inch deep, in a frying pan, add the flautas and fry until lightly browned. Drain on kitchen paper towels.
Cooking time: about 15 minutes
Makes 4

Beef Tostadas

METRIC/IMPERIAL	AMERICAN
8 tortillas, fried (see method)	8 bought tostadas or 8 tortillas, fried (see method)
oil for frying	oil for frying
450 g/1 lb minced beef	1 lb ground beef
1 × 30 g/1¼ oz envelope taco or Chilli con Carne seasoning mix	1 envelope (1¼ oz) taco seasoning mix
175 ml/6 fl oz water	¾ cup water
1 tablespoon vinegar	1 tablespoon vinegar
2 tomatoes, chopped	2 tomatoes, chopped
shredded lettuce	shredded lettuce
grated cheese	grated Monterey Jack cheese
stoned black olives	pitted ripe olives

For the tostadas, heat about 5 mm/¼ inch oil in a frying pan, add the tortillas and fry for about 1 minute on each side until golden brown and crisp. Keep hot. If cooked earlier or bought, wrap the tostadas loosely in foil, place in a preheated cool oven (150°C/300°F, Gas Mark 2) and heat through for 5 to 10 minutes.

Meanwhile place the beef in a large frying pan and fry until brown and cooked, breaking up the meat as it cooks. Pour off any excess fat. Add the seasoning mix, water and vinegar. Bring to the boil, stirring. Stir in tomatoes.

Place a large spoonful of beef mixture on each tostada and top with lettuce, cheese and olives.
Cooking time: 20 minutes
Makes 8

Minced Beef Tacos

METRIC/IMPERIAL	AMERICAN
500 g/1 lb minced beef	1 lb ground beef
50 g/2 oz onion, chopped	½ cup chopped onion
2 teaspoons chilli powder	2 teaspoons chili powder
1 teaspoon crushed oregano leaves	1 teaspoon crushed oregano leaves
1 large clove garlic, crushed	1 large clove garlic, minced
1 × 298 g/10½ oz can condensed beef soup with 1 tablespoon chopped green chilli	1 can (11¼ oz) condensed chili beef soup
4 tablespoons water	¼ cup water
pinch cayenne pepper	generous dash cayenne pepper
12 tacos (see page 40)	12 tacos (see page 40)
Garnish:	**Garnish:**
grated Cheddar cheese	grated Cheddar cheese
shredded lettuce	shredded lettuce
chopped onion	chopped onion
diced tomato	diced tomato
sliced olives	sliced olives

Place the beef, onion, chilli powder, oregano and garlic in a pan and fry until the meat is brown and tender, breaking up the meat as it cooks. Add the beef soup, water and cayenne. Cook over a low heat for 5 minutes, stirring occasionally. Fill each taco with about 4 tablespoons/¼ cup of the meat mixture.

Top the meat with the garnishes.
Cooking time: 20 minutes
Makes 12

Tamales

METRIC/IMPERIAL
225 g/8 oz cornmeal
1 teaspoon salt
¼ teaspoon baking
   powder
100 g/4 oz lard
about 175 ml/6 fl oz
   lukewarm chicken
   stock
18 pieces of non-stick
   or greaseproof
   paper, each 13 ×
   19 cm/5 × 7½ inches
Filling:
chopped green chillies
   and grated cheese
   or chopped cooked
   chicken, or Picadillo
   (see page 28)

AMERICAN
1⅓ cups cornmeal
1 teaspoon salt
¼ teaspoon baking
   powder
½ cup lard
about ¾ cup
   lukewarm chicken
   stock or broth
18 corn husks, soaked
   until pliable, or 18
   pieces parchment
   paper, each 5 ×
   7½ inches
Filling:
chopped green chilies
   and grated cheese
   or chopped cooked
   chicken, or Picadillo
   (see page 28)

Mix the cornmeal with the salt and baking powder. Beat the lard, using an electric mixer, and gradually beat in the cornmeal mixture and chicken stock. Beat for 3 minutes.

For each tamale, spread about 2 tablespoons of the dough in a 7.5 cm/3 inch square on the paper or drained corn husks. Spoon about 2 tablespoons filling in the centre of the dough. Firmly fold the sides of the paper or husks together so the dough meets. Turn in the ends of the paper or husks and tie. Line the top of a steamer with paper or husks. Pack the tamales, tied end up, in the steamer. Cover with more paper or husks and a thick cloth.

Bring the water in the bottom of the steamer to the boil. Cover and simmer for 3 hours.
Cooking time: about 3 hours
Serves 6

Panuchos

METRIC/IMPERIAL
2 onions, sliced
5 tablespoons wine
   vinegar
120 ml/4 fl oz chicken
   stock
½ teaspoon ground
   cumin
½ teaspoon dried
   oregano
1 clove garlic,
   crushed
750 g/1½ lb cooked
   chicken meat, thinly
   sliced
12 freshly prepared
   corn tortillas, fried
   until puffed (see
   page 40)
Refried Beans (see
   page 47)
4 hard-boiled eggs,
   sliced
Red Chilli Sauce (see
   page 40)

AMERICAN
2 onions, sliced
5 tablespoons wine
   vinegar
½ cup chicken stock
   or broth
½ teaspoon ground
   cumin
½ teaspoon dried
   oregano
1 clove garlic, minced
1½ lb cooked chicken
   meat, thinly sliced
12 freshly prepared
   corn tortillas, fried
   until puffed (see
   page 40)
Refried Beans (see
   page 47)
4 hard-cooked eggs,
   sliced
Red Chili Sauce (see
   page 40)

Place the onions, vinegar, chicken stock, cumin, oregano and garlic in a pan. Cover and simmer for 5 minutes. Add the chicken and heat through. Drain if necessary.

Make a slit at the base of each puffed tortilla and open to make a cavity. Fill with about 3 tablespoons of the beans and a few egg slices. Top each panucho with about 2 tablespoons of the chicken mixture and spoon some sauce over.
Cooking time: 10 minutes
Makes 12
Note: if the tortillas will not puff up, spread the beans on to the fried tortillas and top with the egg slices, chicken mixture and sauce.

Tortilla Chips

METRIC/IMPERIAL
thin corn tortillas (see
   page 40)
oil for deep frying

AMERICAN
thin corn tortillas (see
   page 40)
oil for deep frying

Cut each tortilla into 6 equal triangles. Heat the oil to 190°C/375°F. Deep fry the tortilla chips until golden and crisp. Do not overcook. Drain on paper towels.
Cooking time: a few minutes

Salads & Vegetable Dishes

Mexican Salad

METRIC/IMPERIAL	AMERICAN
1 × 425 g/15 oz can red kidney beans	1 can (16 oz) pinto or red kidney beans
4 tablespoons corn oil	¼ cup corn oil
4 corn tortillas	4 corn tortillas
100 g/4 oz lettuce, shredded	2 cups shredded lettuce
4 slices cooked ham, cut into strips	4 slices cooked ham, cut into strips
100 g/4 oz cheese, cut into strips	¼ lb Cheddar cheese, cut into strips
Topopo dressing:	**Topopo dressing:**
150 ml/¼ pint corn oil	⅔ cup corn oil
5 tablespoons wine vinegar	⅓ cup wine vinegar
1 teaspoon salt	1 teaspoon salt
½ teaspoon brown sugar	½ teaspoon brown sugar
½ teaspoon paprika	½ teaspoon paprika
½ teaspoon dry mustard	½ teaspoon dry mustard
¼ teaspoon pepper	¼ teaspoon pepper
⅛ teaspoon Tabasco	⅛ teaspoon hot pepper sauce
Garnish:	**Garnish:**
black olives	ripe olives
red and green chillies	red and green chilies
tiny tomatoes	cherry tomatoes

Coarsely mash the beans with the bean liquid in a medium frying pan. Stir in 2 tablespoons of the corn oil. Cook for about 10 minutes over medium heat, stirring to prevent sticking, until all the liquid is absorbed; set aside. Heat the remaining oil in a pan, add the tortillas and fry over medium heat until lightly browned on

Mexican Salad and some other delicious salad combinations
(Photograph: Mazola Corn Oil)

both sides. Drain on kitchen paper towels.

Place all the ingredients for the dressing in a screw-top jar and shake well. Chill.

Spread the tortillas generously with the beans. Pile the lettuce on the beans. Arrange alternate strips of ham and cheese over the lettuce. Garnish with the olives, chillies and tomatoes. Serve with the chilled dressing.
Serves 4

Refried Beans

METRIC/IMPERIAL	AMERICAN
200 g/7 oz dried pinto beans	1 cup dried pinto beans
¼ onion, diced	¼ onion, diced
1 clove garlic	1 clove garlic
35 g/1¼ oz lard	2½ tablespoons shortening
salt	salt

Place the beans in a large pan and add hot water to cover. Leave to stand overnight or for at least 8 hours. Drain the beans, rinse. Cover with fresh hot water, bring to the boil and boil for 10 minutes. Add the onion and garlic. Partly cover and simmer for 2 hours.

Add 15 g/½ oz (1 tablespoon) of the lard (shortening) and salt to taste. Simmer for a further 2 to 4 hours until the beans are tender. Check the water level during cooking, keeping the beans covered with water.

Melt the remaining lard (shortening) in a frying pan. Using a slotted spoon, put the beans in the pan. Add a little cooking liquid. Mash the beans with a potato masher. Add salt to taste. Simmer the beans to the required consistency, stirring frequently. Serve on their own, as an accompaniment or as a filling.
Cooking time: 4 to 6 hours
Serves 4

Spicy Chick Peas

METRIC/IMPERIAL
300 g/10 oz dried chick peas, soaked overnight in cold water
1½ teaspoons salt
6 rashers streaky bacon, diced
2 onions, chopped
1 clove garlic, crushed
1 red pepper, cored, seeded and chopped
¼ teaspoon ground black pepper
1 small dried hot red chilli, crumbled
½ teaspoon dried oregano
150 g/5 oz canned tomato sauce

AMERICAN
1⅓ cups dried chick peas, soaked overnight in cold water
1½ teaspoons salt
6 bacon slices, diced
2 onions, chopped
1 clove garlic, minced
1 red pepper, seeded and chopped
¼ teaspoon ground black pepper
1 small dried hot red chili, crumbled
½ teaspoon dried oregano
5 oz canned tomato sauce

Drain the chick peas and place in a pan with 1 teaspoon of the salt. Pour over enough water just to cover. Bring to the boil, boil for 10 minutes and simmer, uncovered, for about 45 minutes until the chick peas are cooked and tender. Drain.

Place the bacon in a pan and fry until the fat runs. Add the onions, garlic and red pepper and fry until soft. Stir in the remaining salt, the black pepper, chilli, oregano, tomato sauce and chick peas. Simmer for 10 minutes, stirring occasionally.

Cooking time: about 1¼ hours
Serves 4

Mexican Rice

METRIC/IMPERIAL
225 g/8 oz long-grain rice
4 tablespoons oil
1 small onion, grated
1 clove garlic, crushed
1 green or red pepper, cored, seeded and chopped
1 large tomato, skinned, seeded and chopped (optional)
1 tablespoon finely chopped coriander or parsley
1 tablespoon ground cumin
600-750 ml/1-1¼ pints rich chicken or beef stock
salt and freshly ground pepper

AMERICAN
1 cup long-grain rice
¼ cup oil
1 small onion, minced
1 clove garlic, minced
1 green or red pepper, seeded and chopped
1 large tomato, peeled, seeded and chopped (optional)
1 tablespoon finely chopped coriander or parsley
1 tablespoon ground cumin
2½-3 cups rich chicken or beef stock
salt and freshly ground pepper

Place the rice in a sieve and rinse thoroughly with cold running water to remove excess starch. Cover with hot water and leave to stand for 30 minutes, then drain. Leave in the sieve for about 1 hour until dry.

Heat the oil in a heavy frying pan, add the rice and cook, stirring, over a low heat until all the rice grains are well coated with oil. Add the onion and cook until it is transparent and the rice is golden.

Mix in the garlic, chopped pepper, tomato, if using, coriander or parsley and cumin. Add the stock. Cover tightly and cook over a low heat for 20 to 30 minutes or until the liquid is absorbed and the rice is tender and fluffy.

If softer rice is preferred, add a little more stock after 20 minutes and continue cooking until the additional liquid is absorbed.

Add salt and pepper to taste and serve hot as a snack, or as an accompaniment to a main course dish.

Cooking time: 40 minutes
Serves 4 to 6

Chilli Rellenos

METRIC/IMPERIAL
6 large California
  chillies, roasted and
  skinned (see
  method), or use
  canned
oil or lard for frying
175 g/6 oz Cheddar
  cheese, cut into
  25 g/1 oz sticks
3 eggs, separated
50 g/2 oz plain flour
Red Chilli Sauce (see
  page 40)
50 g/2 oz Cheddar
  cheese, grated

AMERICAN
6 California chilies,
  roasted and peeled
  (see method), or
  use canned
oil or shortening for
  frying
6 oz Monterey Jack
  cheese, cut into
  1 oz sticks
3 eggs, separated
½ cup all-purpose
  flour
Red Chili Sauce (see
  page 40)
½ cup grated
  Monterey Jack
  cheese

To peel the chillies: heat oil or lard (shortening) in a deep fryer to 180°C/350°F. Add the whole chillies and allow to blister. Turn over so the blisters form on all sides. Remove, allow to cool, then peel off the skin.

Cut a small slit in each chilli and remove the seeds, leaving on the stems. Dry well with kitchen paper towels. Place a stick of cheese in each chilli. Beat the egg whites until stiff. Lightly beat the egg yolks. Add the yolks to the white all at once and fold in lightly. Roll the chillies in the flour, then dip into the egg mixture to coat.

Heat the oil or lard (shortening) in a deep fryer to 180°C/350°F. Add the coated chillies and fry until brown, then turn and fry on the other side. (The chillies should float on the oil.) Drain on kitchen paper towels. Put the chillies in a shallow flameproof dish and top with the sauce and cheese. Place under a preheated grill (broiler) to melt the cheese.

Other fillings may be used, such as Picadillo (see page 28) or Refried Beans (see page 47).
Cooking time: about 15 minutes
Serves 3 to 6

Kidney Bean Stew

METRIC/IMPERIAL
225 g/8 oz dried red
  kidney beans
1 onion, halved
1½ teaspoons
  chopped coriander
25 g/1 oz lard or
  bacon fat
1 chilli, skinned and
  chopped (optional)
1 small tomato,
  skinned and
  chopped (optional)
salt
crumbled Cheddar
  cheese to garnish

AMERICAN
1⅓ cups dried red
  kidney beans
1 onion, halved
1½ teaspoons
  chopped coriander
2 tablespoons
  shortening or
  bacon fat
1 chili serrano, peeled
  and chopped
  (optional)
1 small tomato,
  peeled and
  chopped (optional)
salt
crumbled farmer's
  cheese or strips of
  Monterey Jack for
  garnish

Rinse the beans thoroughly in cold water. Place in a large saucepan and cover with cold water. Grate or mince half of the onion. Add to the beans with the coriander, lard (shortening) and, if used, the chilli and tomato.

Bring to the boil, boil for 10 minutes and lower the heat. Cover tightly and simmer gently for 1 to 1½ hours until just tender. Add salt to taste, stir well and cook gently for a further 20 to 30 minutes. Remove from the heat and leave to stand for several hours to allow the flavour to develop.

Before serving, reheat thoroughly, stirring all the time. Slice the other onion half. Garnish the stew with the onion slices and cheese.

Mexicans eat this stew immediately after the main course of the meal, served in small bowls.
Cooking time: 1½ to 2 hours
Serves 4

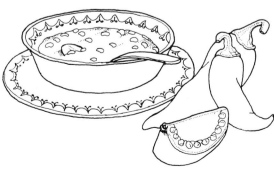

Marrow (Squash) with Tomatoes and Cheese

METRIC/IMPERIAL
75 g/3 oz unsalted
  butter or
  6 tablespoons
  olive oil
1 small clove garlic,
  crushed
1 large onion, finely
  chopped
750 g/1½ lb marrow
  or courgettes, diced
2 tomatoes, skinned,
  seeded and
  coarsely chopped
1 small red chilli,
  skinned, seeded
  and chopped
salt
100 g/4 oz mild
  Cheddar or Gruyère
  cheese, grated
25 g/1 oz fresh
  breadcrumbs

AMERICAN
6 tablespoons
  unsalted butter or
  olive oil
1 small clove garlic,
  minced
1 large onion, finely
  chopped
1½ lb squash or
  zucchini, diced
2 tomatoes, peeled,
  seeded and
  coarsely chopped
1 small chili serrano,
  skinned, seeded
  and chopped
salt
1 cup grated mild
  Cheddar or Gruyère
  cheese
½ cup soft bread
  crumbs

Lightly grease a gratin dish or shallow ovenproof dish. Heat two-thirds of the butter or oil in a heavy frying pan, add the garlic and onion and fry until transparent but not brown.

Stir in the marrow (squash) or courgettes (zucchini), tomatoes, chilli and salt to taste. Cover and cook over a low heat for about 10 minutes or until the marrow (squash) or courgettes (zucchini) are tender but not soft, shaking the pan occasionally to prevent the vegetables sticking.

Spoon the mixture into the prepared dish. Mix the cheese and breadcrumbs together and sprinkle over the vegetables. Dot with the remaining butter or oil. Place under a preheated grill (broiler) for 3 to 5 minutes.

Alternatively, cook in a preheated moderately hot oven (200°C/400°F, Gas Mark 6) and cook for about 10 minutes until the top is crisp and golden brown.
Cooking time: 20 to 30 minutes
Serves 6

Huevos Rancheros

METRIC/IMPERIAL
oil for frying
4 corn or flour
  tortillas (see page
  40)
1 onion, chopped
1 clove garlic,
  crushed
1 × 425 g/15 oz can
  tomatoes, chopped
2 × 100 g/4 oz cans
  chopped green
  chillies or 4 fresh
  chillies, seeded and
  chopped
¾ teaspoon salt
4 eggs
⅛ teaspoon pepper
100 g/4 oz Cheddar
  cheese, grated
50 g/2 oz butter,
  melted

AMERICAN
oil for frying
4 corn or flour
  tortillas (see page
  40)
½ cup chopped onion
1 clove garlic,
  minced
1 × 14 oz can
  tomatoes, chopped
2 cans (4 oz each)
  chopped green
  chilies
¾ teaspoon salt
4 eggs
⅛ teaspoon pepper
1 cup grated Cheddar
  cheese
¼ cup melted butter

Heat 2.5 cm/1 inch of oil in a pan and fry the tortillas until crispy. Line a shallow casserole dish with the tortillas.

Heat 2 tablespoons oil in a pan and cook the onion and garlic until soft. Stir in the tomatoes, green chillies and ½ teaspoon salt. Pour this mixture over the tortillas. Carefully break the eggs, one on top of each tortilla. Sprinkle remaining salt, pepper and the cheese over eggs. Pour over melted butter and cover. Cook in a preheated moderate oven (180°C/350°F, Gas Mark 4) for 15 minutes. Serve immediately.
Cooking time: 35 minutes
Serves 4

Huevos Rancheros
(Photograph: Old El Paso Products)

Rice Salad Olé!

METRIC/IMPERIAL	AMERICAN
225 g/8 oz cooked chicken, cut into strips	1 cup sliced cooked chicken
275 g/10 oz cooked long-grain rice	2 cups cooked long-grain rice
25 g/1 oz onion, finely chopped	1/4 cup finely chopped onion
2 tablespoons oil	2 tablespoons oil
2 tablespoons vinegar	2 tablespoons vinegar
1 teaspoon salt	1 teaspoon salt
1/2 teaspoon Tabasco	1/2 teaspoon hot pepper sauce
2 tomatoes, diced	2 tomatoes, diced
1 small lettuce, finely shredded	1 small head lettuce, finely shredded
50 g/2 oz tortilla chips (see page 45)	2 cups tortilla chips (see page 45)

Combine the cooked chicken, rice, onion, oil, vinegar, salt, Tabasco (hot pepper) sauce, tomatoes and lettuce together. Chill.

Just before serving, add the tortilla chips and toss lightly.
Serves 6

Latin Seafood Salad

METRIC/IMPERIAL	AMERICAN
50 g/2 oz Cheddar cheese, grated	1/2 cup grated Cheddar cheese
65 g/2 1/2 oz pimento-stuffed olives, sliced	1/2 cup sliced pimiento-stuffed olives
5 tablespoons soured cream	1/3 cup sour cream
2 tablespoons finely chopped onion	1/4 cup minced onion
1 teaspoon garlic salt	1 teaspoon garlic salt
3/4 teaspoon chilli powder	3/4 teaspoon chili powder
2 × 198 g/7 oz cans tuna chunks, drained	1 can (12 1/2 oz) tuna chunks, drained
crisp salad greens	crisp salad greens
1 large avocado, halved, stoned and peeled	1 large avocado, halved, pitted and peeled
2 medium tomatoes, cut into wedges	2 medium-size tomatoes, cut into wedges
paprika	paprika
tortilla chips, to serve (see page 45)	tortilla chips, to serve (see page 45)

Mix the cheese, olives, soured cream, onion, garlic salt and chilli powder together. Fold in the tuna. Line 4 salad plates with crisp salad greens. Mound the tuna mixture on to the salad. Cut the avocado into wedges. Arrange avocado and tomato around tuna. Sprinkle with paprika and serve with tortilla chips.
Serves 4

Mixed Meat Salad

METRIC/IMPERIAL	AMERICAN
300 ml/1/2 pint fresh chicken stock	1 can (10 3/4 oz) condensed chicken broth
120 ml/4 fl oz oil	1/2 cup oil
5 tablespoons wine vinegar	1/3 cup wine vinegar
1/2 teaspoon sugar	1/2 teaspoon sugar
1 teaspoon crushed marjoram leaves	1 teaspoon crushed marjoram leaves
1/2 teaspoon crushed oregano leaves	1/2 teaspoon crushed oregano leaves
1/2 teaspoon crushed thyme leaves	1/2 teaspoon crushed thyme leaves
good pinch cayenne pepper	generous dash cayenne pepper
350 g/12 oz cooked beef, cut into strips	1 1/2 cups cooked beef, cut into strips
225 g/8 oz cooked chicken, cut into strips	1 cup cooked chicken, cut into strips
225 g/8 oz cooked ham, cut into strips	1 cup cooked ham, cut into strips
1 medium green pepper, cored, seeded and cut into strips	1 medium-size green pepper, seeded and cut into strips
1 medium red pepper, cored, seeded and cut into strips	1 medium-size red pepper, seeded and cut into strips
1 onion, thinly sliced	1 onion, thinly sliced
40 g/1 1/2 oz pimento-stuffed olives, thinly sliced	1/4 cup thinly sliced pimiento-stuffed olives

Place the chicken stock or broth, oil, vinegar, sugar, herbs and cayenne in a pan and heat, stirring occasionally.

Meanwhile arrange the meats, peppers, onion and olives in a shallow dish. Pour the herb mixture over. Cover and chill for 6 hours or more, stirring occasionally.

Drain the meats and serve with a green salad.
Serves 4 to 6

Fiesta Salad

METRIC/IMPERIAL	AMERICAN
450 g/1 lb cooked rice	3 cups cooked rice
450 g/1 lb cooked chicken, chopped	2 cups chopped cooked chicken
50 g/2 oz Cheddar cheese, grated	½ cup grated Monterey Jack cheese
100 g/4 oz celery, sliced diagonally	1 cup diagonally sliced celery
1 onion, sliced	1 small onion, thinly sliced
½ green pepper, cored, seeded and cut into strips	½ green pepper, seeded and cut into strips
1 × 100 g/4 oz can green chillies, diced	1 can (4 oz) green chilies, diced
1 clove garlic, crushed	1 clove garlic, minced
2 teaspoons chilli powder	2 teaspoons chili powder
1½ teaspoons salt	1½ teaspoons salt
120 ml/4 fl oz soured cream	½ cup sour cream
stoned black olives, to garnish	pitted ripe olives, for garnish

Combine all the ingredients, except the olives, in a large salad bowl and toss lightly. Garnish with olives and serve on salad greens.
Serves 6

Christmas Salad

METRIC/IMPERIAL	AMERICAN
1 Cos lettuce	1 head Romaine lettuce
2 small cooked beetroots, skinned and diced	2 small cooked beets, peeled and diced
1 large cooked carrot, diced	1 large cooked carrot, diced
1 orange, peeled and chopped	1 orange, peeled and chopped
1 cooking apple, peeled and diced	1 baking apple, peeled and diced
¼ fresh pineapple, peeled, cored and diced	¼ fresh pineapple, peeled, cored and diced
1 large banana, diced	1 large banana, diced
Dressing:	**Dressing:**
1 tablespoon lime or lemon juice	1 tablespoon lime or lemon juice
3 tablespoons salad oil	3 tablespoons salad oil
½ teaspoon sugar	½ teaspoon sugar
¼ teaspoon salt	¼ teaspoon salt

Garnish:	Garnish:
50 g/2 oz walnuts, almonds or unsalted peanuts, chopped	½ cup chopped walnuts, almonds or unsalted peanuts
seeds of ½ small pomegranate	seeds of ½ small pomegranate

Use half of the lettuce leaves to line a salad bowl. Shred the remaining lettuce and mix with the beetroots (beets), carrot and fruits.

To make the dressing: put the lime or lemon juice, salad oil, sugar, and the salt into a screw-top jar. Shake vigorously until thoroughly blended and the sugar is dissolved. Pour the dressing over the fruit salad and toss well.

Pile the salad into the salad bowl and garnish with the nuts and pomegranate seeds. Serve chilled.
Serves 6
Illustrated on page 35

Ranchero Bread

METRIC/IMPERIAL	AMERICAN
150 g/5 oz cornmeal	1 cup cornmeal
1 teaspoon salt	1 teaspoon salt
½ teaspoon bicarbonate of soda	½ teaspoon baking soda
250 ml/8 fl oz milk	1 cup milk
2 eggs, beaten	2 eggs, beaten
4 tablespoons oil	¼ cup oil
300 g/11 oz cooked rice	2 cups cooked rice
1 × 525 g/17 oz can cream-style corn	1 can (17 oz) cream-style corn
50 g/2 oz onion, finely chopped	½ cup finely chopped onion
2 tablespoons finely chopped jalapeno or other chilli	2 tablespoons finely chopped jalapeno chili or 1 can (4 oz) diced green chilies
225 g/8 oz Cheddar cheese, grated	2 cups grated Cheddar cheese

Sift the cornmeal, salt and soda together into a large mixing bowl. Add the milk, eggs, oil, rice, corn, onion, chilli and cheese, stirring only to blend well. Pour into a 30 cm/12 inch cake tin or ovenproof frying pan which has been greased and sprinkled with cornmeal.

Cook in a preheated moderate oven (180°C/350°F, Gas Mark 4) for 40 to 45 minutes.
Cooking time: 40 to 45 minutes
Serves 8 to 10

Desserts & Drinks

Mangoes with Cream

METRIC/IMPERIAL	AMERICAN
250 ml/8 fl oz water	1 cup water
100 g/4 oz sugar	½ cup sugar
small piece of cinnamon stick	small piece of cinnamon stick
3 mangoes, peeled and thickly sliced lengthways	3 mangoes, peeled and thickly sliced lengthwise
½ teaspoon vanilla essence	½ teaspoon vanilla extract
150 ml/¼ pint double cream	⅔ cup heavy cream
4 tablespoons rum or dry sherry	¼ cup rum or pale dry sherry

Combine the water, half of the sugar and the cinnamon stick in a heavy pan. Bring to the boil, then simmer for about 20 to 30 minutes, stirring occasionally, until the syrup thickens.

Add the mango slices to the syrup and simmer for 7 to 10 minutes until tender but not mushy. Discard the cinnamon stick. Add the vanilla. Allow to cool, then chill for at least 1 hour.

Just before serving, whip the cream with the remaining sugar and fold in the rum or sherry. Spoon the fruit into individual serving dishes. Pour over a little of the syrup and top with swirls of cream.

Cooking time: 45 minutes

Serves 4

Note: fresh pineapple is equally delicious prepared and cooked in this way.

Fiesta Snowballs

METRIC/IMPERIAL	AMERICAN
225 g/8 oz cooking fat	1·cup shortening
1 teaspoon vanilla essence	1 teaspoon vanilla extract
1 teaspoon grated lemon rind	1 teaspoon grated lemon rind
100 g/4 oz caster sugar	½ cup sugar
¼ teaspoon salt	¼ teaspoon salt
100 g/4 oz wheat germ	¾ cup vacuum packed wheat germ (regular)
175 g/6 oz plain flour	1½ cups all-purpose flour
icing sugar	confectioners' sugar

Beat the fat, vanilla, lemon rind, sugar and salt until soft and fluffy. Mix in the wheat germ and flour. Press the dough with the fingers until it holds together. Shape the dough into 2.5 cm/ 1 inch balls (to shape balls of the same size, divide the dough into quarters and roll 9 balls from each quarter). Place on ungreased baking sheets.

Cook in a preheated moderate oven (180°C/350°F, Gas Mark 4) for 12 to 15 minutes. While hot, roll in icing (confectioners') sugar. Cool on a wire tray. If liked, roll in icing (confectioners') sugar again.

Cooking time: 12 to 15 minutes

Makes 36

Mangoes with Cream

Sweet Pumpkin Dessert

METRIC/IMPERIAL	AMERICAN
1 kg/2 lb pumpkin, peeled	2 lb pumpkin, peeled
4 tablespoons water	¼ cup water
275 g/10 oz dark brown sugar	1⅔ cups dark brown sugar

Remove the fibres and seeds from the pumpkin. Cut into 8 equal pieces. Pour the water into a shallow flameproof casserole or deep frying pan and arrange the pumpkin pieces in one layer in the dish or pan. Sprinkle thickly with the sugar. Cover and simmer for about 50 minutes, basting occasionally, until the pumpkin is tender but still retains its shape. Remove from the heat and leave to cool.

Transfer the pumpkin pieces to a serving dish using a slotted spoon. Spoon over the syrupy cooking liquid. Serve with whipped cream.
Cooking time: about 50 minutes
Serves 4

Bananas with Rum

METRIC/IMPERIAL	AMERICAN
40 g/1½ oz butter	3 tablespoons butter
40 g/1½ oz brown sugar	3 tablespoons brown sugar
20 g/¾ oz sugar	2 tablespoons sugar
100 g/4 oz canned and drained pineapple chunks	⅔ cup canned and drained pineapple chunks
2 large bananas, sliced diagonally	2 large bananas, sliced diagonally
about 120 ml/4 fl oz rum	½ cup rum
vanilla ice cream to serve	vanilla ice cream to serve

Melt the butter in a pan over a low heat. Stir in the sugars until dissolved. Add the pineapple and bananas and turn to coat in the syrup. Heat until bubbling. Add the rum and ignite. Either serve flaming over the ice cream or wait until the flames have subsided.
Cooking time: about 5 minutes
Serves 4

Mexican Almond Pudding

METRIC/IMPERIAL	AMERICAN
½ envelope gelatine	1 envelope unflavored gelatin
2½ tablespoons water	2½ tablespoons water
3 eggs, separated	3 eggs, separated
75 g/3 oz caster sugar	¼ cup plus 2 tablespoons sugar
¼ teaspoon almond essence	¼ teaspoon almond extract
½ teaspoon finely grated orange rind	½ teaspoon finely grated orange rind
4 drops red food colouring	4 drops red food coloring
4 drops green food colouring	4 drops green food coloring
175 ml/6 fl oz milk	¾ cup milk
few drops vanilla essence	few drops vanilla extract
2 tablespoons slivered almonds, toasted	2 tablespoons slivered almonds, toasted

Sprinkle the gelatine over the water in a small pan. Stir over a low heat until the gelatine has dissolved. Cool at room temperature for 15 minutes until syrupy. Do not allow to set. Mix the gelatine with the egg whites and beat until foamy. Add 50 g/2 oz (¼ cup) of the sugar gradually, beating continuously. Beat until soft peaks form. Beat in the almond essence (extract) and orange rind. Divide into 3 equal portions. Colour 1 portion pink and 1 portion green, using the food colourings. Chill all 3 portions.

Mix the egg yolks, remaining sugar and milk in the top of a double boiler or in a heatproof bowl over a pan of simmering water. Cook, stirring, until the custard thickens and coats the back of a spoon. Add the vanilla. Cover the surface and chill.

To serve, place a scoop of each colour pudding in 4 individual dishes. Top with 3 tablespoons of the custard. Sprinkle with almonds.
Cooking time: about 20 minutes
Serves 4

Bunuelos

METRIC/IMPERIAL
225 g/8 oz plain flour
½ teaspoon baking
   powder
pinch of salt
1 tablespoon sugar
1 egg, well beaten
25 g/1 oz lard,
   unsalted butter or
   margarine, melted
about 120 ml/4 fl oz
   milk
oil for deep frying
Syrup:
350 ml/12 fl oz water
4 tablespoons sherry
115 g/4½ oz dark
   brown sugar
½ cinnamon stick or
   ¼ teaspoon ground
   cinnamon

AMERICAN
2 cups all-purpose
   flour
½ teaspoon baking
   powder
pinch of salt
1 tablespoon sugar
1 egg, well beaten
2 tablespoons melted
   shortening,
   unsalted butter or
   margarine
about ½ cup milk
oil for deep frying
Syrup:
1½ cups water
¼ cup sherry
¾ cup dark brown
   sugar
½ cinnamon stick or
   ¼ teaspoon ground
   cinnamon

Sift the flour, baking powder and salt into a large bowl. Stir in the sugar. Add the egg, fat and just enough milk to form a soft, but not too sticky dough. Turn out on to a floured board and knead until smooth and pliable.

Divide the dough into 8 to 12 equal-sized pieces. With moistened hands, shape each one into a ball. Cover with a sheet of cling film (plastic wrap) and leave to stand for 30 minutes. Shape the balls into flat cakes on a floured surface. Make a shallow depression in the centre of each one.

Heat the oil to 190°C/375°F. Fry the cakes, a few at a time, until golden brown and puffy. Drain on kitchen paper towels.

Meanwhile place all the ingredients for the syrup in a heavy pan. Bring slowly to the boil, stirring. Simmer, stirring occasionally, for 20 to 30 minutes until the mixture thickens. Discard the cinnamon stick.

Serve the fritters as a dessert or snack. Place in bowls and accompany with plenty of syrup.
Cooking time: 30 minutes
Serves 4 to 6

Mexican Bread and Honey Dessert

METRIC/IMPERIAL
4 slices white bread,
   crusts removed and
   cut into large strips
120 ml/4 fl oz milk
1 egg, lightly beaten
25 g/1 oz butter
4 tablespoons clear
   honey
4 tablespoons dry
   sherry

AMERICAN
4 slices white bread,
   crusts removed and
   cut into large strips
½ cup milk
1 egg, lightly beaten
2 tablespoons butter
4 tablespoons clear
   honey
¼ cup dry sherry

Place the bread in a shallow dish and pour over the milk. Leave to soak for 4 minutes. Using a slotted spoon, transfer the bread to kitchen paper towels to drain. Dip the bread in the beaten egg, then put on a plate.

Melt the butter in a flameproof casserole, add the bread and fry until lightly browned. Mix the honey and sherry together and pour into the casserole. Cook in a preheated moderate oven (160°C/325°F, Gas Mark 3) for 20 to 25 minutes until golden brown. Serve hot or cold.
Cooking time: about 35 minutes
Serves 2 to 3

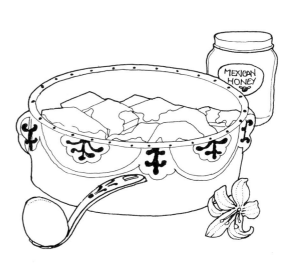

Bread Pudding Mexican Style

METRIC/IMPERIAL
250 ml/8 fl oz water
225 g/8 oz dark brown sugar
1½ teaspoons ground cinnamon
50 g/2 oz butter
10 slices stale bread, crusts removed and cubed
50 g/2 oz sultanas
100 g/4 oz walnuts, chopped
175 g/6 oz cottage cheese

AMERICAN
1 cup water
1⅓ cups dark brown sugar
1½ teaspoons ground cinnamon
¼ cup butter
10 slices stale bread, crusts removed and cubed
⅓ cup golden raisins or raisins
1 cup chopped walnuts
¾ cup cottage cheese

Place the water, sugar and half of the cinnamon in a pan and heat, stirring continuously, until the sugar has melted. Cook the mixture for 5 minutes, without stirring.

Melt the butter in a large frying pan, add the bread cubes and fry until evenly browned. Remove from the heat and stir in the syrup. Add the sultanas (golden raisins), walnuts and cottage cheese. Simmer until the ingredients are well blended.

Transfer the mixture to a well-greased ovenproof dish and sprinkle over the remaining cinnamon. Cook in a preheated moderately hot oven (190°C/375°F, Gas Mark 5) for 15 to 20 minutes until set and golden brown. Serve warm with whipped cream.
Cooking time: about 40 minutes
Serves 4

Mexican Caramel Custard

METRIC/IMPERIAL
225 g/8 oz sugar
900 ml/1½ pints milk
pinch of salt
1 vanilla pod, or 1 teaspoon vanilla essence, dry sherry or rum
1 cinnamon stick (optional)
3 eggs
6 egg yolks
Decoration:
150 ml/¼ pint cream, whipped
blanched almonds, toasted and crushed

AMERICAN
1 cup sugar
3¾ cups milk
pinch of salt
1 vanilla bean, or 1 teaspoon vanilla extract, pale dry sherry or rum
1 cinnamon stick (optional)
3 eggs
6 egg yolks
Decoration:
⅔ cup whipped cream
almonds, toasted and crushed

Place half of the sugar in a heavy frying pan over low heat and stir gently until melted and transparent. Boil briskly, without stirring, until the syrup turns golden. Pour a little caramel into 6 dariole moulds or custard cups, turning the moulds until evenly coated, part way up.

Heat the milk in a heavy pan over a low heat. Add the remaining sugar, the salt, vanilla, sherry or rum and cinnamon stick, if used. Cook, stirring frequently, for 2 to 3 minutes. Allow to cool and remove cinnamon stick.

Beat the eggs and egg yolks together until frothy, then stir in the milk. Strain the custard and pour into the prepared moulds.

Place the moulds in a roasting pan, containing about 2.5 cm/1 inch hot water. Cover the moulds with buttered greaseproof (waxed) paper. Cook in a preheated moderate oven (180°C/350°F, Gas Mark 4) for about 45 minutes or until a knife inserted into the centre of the custard comes out clean. Allow to cool, then chill.

To unmould, dip into hot water and stand for a few minutes. Shake the moulds gently to loosen the custard and turn out on to individual plates. Decorate with cream and almonds.
Cooking time: about 1 hour
Serves 6
Variation:
Chocolate Caramel Custard: grind 25 g/1 oz (1 square) sweetened chocolate in a blender with 250 ml/8 fl oz (1 cup) strong black coffee. Use only 600 ml/1 pint (2½ cups) milk. Add the coffee to the milk and continue as above.

Mexican Caramel Custard

Spiced Chocolate Drink

METRIC/IMPERIAL	AMERICAN
4 cups milk (see note)	4 cups milk (see note)
175 g/6 oz chocolate, coarsely grated (see note)	6 squares chocolate, coarsely grated (see note)
ground cinnamon	ground cinnamon
ground cloves	ground cloves

Place the milk in a pan and heat until lukewarm. Add the chocolate with a pinch each of the spices; stir constantly until the chocolate has melted. Continue stirring over a low heat for 3 to 5 minutes. Remove from the heat and whisk until frothy.

Pour into cups and sprinkle with a little ground cinnamon and ground cloves before serving hot. Alternatively, cool and serve chilled.

Cooking time: about 8 minutes

Serves 4

Note: if preferred, water, or half water and half milk, may be used instead.

Mexican chocolate is ground with nuts, spices and sugar, making a distinctive drink. Locally this is whipped frothy with a molinillo (wooden mill). Any good quality sweetened chocolate can be used for this recipe.

Mexican-Style Coffee

METRIC/IMPERIAL	AMERICAN
4 cups water	4 cups water
1 small cinnamon stick	1 small cinnamon stick
2 cloves	2 cloves
50 g/2 oz dark brown sugar	⅓ cup piloncillo or other dark brown sugar
4 tablespoons freshly ground coffee	4 tablespoons freshly ground coffee

Place the water in a pan or flameproof coffee pot and bring to the boil, add the cinnamon and cloves. Lower the heat, add the sugar and stir constantly until dissolved. Stir in the coffee and simmer for 3 to 5 minutes. Turn off the heat and allow to stand for about 5 minutes, or until the coffee grounds have settled. Remove cinnamon stick and cloves before serving.

Cooking time: about 10 minutes

Serves 4

Acapulco Sunrise

METRIC/IMPERIAL	AMERICAN
4 tablespoons Tequila	¼ cup Tequila
1 tablespoon lime juice	1 tablespoon lime juice
1 tablespoon Curaçao	1 tablespoon Curaçao
1 teaspoon crème de cassis	1 teaspoon crème de cassis
200 ml/⅓ pint soda water	1 cup club soda
lime slice to decorate	lime slice for decoration

Place the Tequila, lime juice, Curaçao, crème de cassis and crushed ice in a cocktail shaker or mixing glass and shake well. Half fill a tall glass with ice. Strain the mixture into the glass. Top up with the soda. Stir, and decorate with the lime slice.

Serves 1

Berta

METRIC/IMPERIAL	AMERICAN
3 tablespoons Tequila	3 tablespoons Tequila
3 tablespoons lemon juice	3 tablespoons lemon juice
3 tablespoons sugar syrup (see method)	3 tablespoons sugar syrup (see method)
soda water	club soda
lemon slice to decorate	lemon slice for decoration

Place some ice in a tall glass. Pour in the Tequila, lemon juice and syrup. Fill the glass with soda and stir. Decorate with the lemon slice.

To make the sugar syrup: place equal amounts of sugar and water in a pan. Bring to the boil so that the sugar dissolves. Refrigerate and use as directed in drinks and cocktail recipes.

Serves 1

White Wine Sangria

METRIC/IMPERIAL	AMERICAN
150 g/5 oz sugar	⅔ cup sugar
450 ml/¾ pint water	2 cups water
1 pineapple, peeled, cored and cut into spears	1 pineapple, peeled, cored and cut into spears
2 limes, thinly sliced	2 limes, thinly sliced
1 orange, thinly sliced	1 orange, thinly sliced
2 bottles Chablis or other dry white wine	2 bottles Chablis or other dry white wine

Place the sugar and water in a pan over a medium heat and stir continuously until the sugar dissolves. When the syrup begins to boil, remove from the heat. Add the pineapple, limes and orange. Leave for at least 4 hours at room temperature.

Place ice in the base of a punch bowl or jugs. Pour over the fruit, syrup and white wine. Stir well and serve.
Serves 8

Sangria

METRIC/IMPERIAL	AMERICAN
1 litre/1¾ pints Spanish red wine	1 quart Spanish red wine
120 ml/4 fl oz good brandy	½ cup good brandy
120 ml/4 fl oz Triple Sec or Cointreau	½ cup Triple Sec or Cointreau
120 ml/4 fl oz soda water	½ cup club soda
1 tablespoon sugar	1 tablespoon sugar
sliced bananas	sliced bananas
sliced lemons	sliced lemons
sliced oranges	sliced oranges

Mix the wine, brandy, liqueur, soda and sugar together in a large jug. Add the fruit and serve over ice.
Serves 6 to 8

Tequila Sunrise

METRIC/IMPERIAL	AMERICAN
3 tablespoons Tequila	3 tablespoons Tequila
1 tablespoon lime juice	1 tablespoon lime juice
6 tablespoons unsweetened orange juice	6 tablespoons unsweetened orange juice
1 tablespoon grenadine	1 tablespoon grenadine
lime slice to decorate	lime slice for decoration

Combine the Tequila, lime and orange juices. Place some ice in a tall glass and pour in the Tequila mixture. Add the grenadine. Decorate with a slice of lime.
Serves 1

Margarita

METRIC/IMPERIAL	AMERICAN
strip of lime or lemon rind	strip of lime or lemon rind
salt	salt
juice of ½ lime or lemon	juice of ½ lime or lemon
4 tablespoons Tequila	4 tablespoons Tequila
1 tablespoon Triple Sec or Cointreau	1 tablespoon Triple Sec or Cointreau
1 slice of lime or lemon, to serve	1 slice of lime or lemon, to serve

Rub the rim of a chilled cocktail glass with the lime or lemon rind then dip in salt. Place some crushed ice in a cocktail shaker or mixing glass. Pour in the lime or lemon juice, Tequila and liqueur. Shake well then strain into the cocktail glass. Top with a lime or lemon slice.
Serves 1

Glossary

Albondigas
Meat balls, usually cooked in a sauce, soup or broth

Ancho
Ripe and dried Poblano chilli

Bunuelos
Fried sweet tortillas

Burritos
Flour tortilla wrapped around a filling, can be covered in sauce and cheese

Chimichangas
Fried burritos

Chipotle
Name of a ripened, dried and smoked chilli

Chorizo
Hard, spicy pork sausage. If unavailable, use pepperoni or other firm, spicy garlic sausage

Cilantro
Fresh coriander leaves, similar to parsley

Enchilada
Corn tortilla rolled around a filling, topped with sauce and cheese, then baked

Epazote
Strong-flavoured herb

Flauta
Two overlapping corn tortillas, filled and rolled to form a long tube, then fried

Guacamole
Seasoned, mashed avocado

Jalapeno
Small, hot, dark green chilli

Mole
Rich sauce cooked with chillies, spices and sometimes chocolate

Nachos
Appetizer made of tortilla chips, topped with chillies, cheese and sauce; baked or grilled (broiled)

Panuchos
Small, puffed tortillas stuffed with filling

Picadillo
Savoury minced (ground) beef mixture, which can be used on its own or as a filling for tacos, enchiladas, etc.

Poblano
Name of a large, green, mildly hot chilli

Quesadilla
Filled tortilla turnover, toasted or fried

Taco
A soft or crisp tortilla shell with a filling. (Commercially prepared taco shells and taco seasoning are available.)

Tamale
Corn dough, spread on corn husks or paper, filled and steamed

Tomatillos
Mexican sweet green tomatoes. Very different from ordinary tomatoes

Tortilla
Traditional flat, unleavened 'bread' made from corn or wheat flour. Served in a variety of ways – plain or buttered; filled and rolled; folded and fried

Tortilla chips *(Tostaditas)*
Small triangular pieces of crispy fried corn tortilla used as garnish and for dipping

Tostada
Crisply fried, flat tortilla topped with a selection of meat, cheese, beans and salad

Index

The publishers would like to acknowledge Robert Golden for the photographs on pages 11; 35; 38; 43; 54 and 59. Illustrations by Susan Neale.

Recipes for this book have been contributed by Old El Paso Products; American Spice Trade Association; US National Live Stock and Meat Board; US National Marine Fisheries Service; Castle & Cooke Foods; Campbell Soup Company; Uncle Ben's Rice Inc; Open Pit Barbecue Sauce; Bird's Eye; R. T. French Company; Californian Iceberg Lettuce Commission; Rice Council; Mazola Corn Oil.